# The Gloomy light

*by*

# Carl Robinson

The Gloomy Light

Part I

IN WHICH PHILOMEL SINGS

Sherwood Park is twelve miles from Washington. Beginning as a fairly bombastic suburb on the primary line of a railroad, it was honored with simple openness until infringing streetcars cleared the tide of settlement away from it, and left it stranded — its train administration, unfit to rival present day engine vehicles, progressively wasteful. Property estimations, unavoidably, diminished. The little suburb declined, and became less elegant. Individuals who could have added social shine to its get-togethers moved away. The casing houses, which at first had made such a daring appearance, turned into a chomped down at the heel. The greater part of them, working before the recovery of good desire for engineering, appeared to be unbalanced and dull with their impersonation towers, their worried overhangs, their dim and brown shading, their groups of differentiating shingles tied like bands around their middles.

The Barnes cabin was saved from the widespread absence of exquisiteness by its basic lines, its white paint and green blinds. However the paint had stripped in places, and the substantial advances which followed the line of the two patios were broken and worn. Old Baldwin Barnes had purchased his home on the portion plan, and his youngsters were all the while paying for it. Old Baldwin had capitulated to the dangerous repetitiveness of composing similar engraving on red falls through thirty years of steadfast help in the Pension Office, and had abandoned the world with his obligations to him.

He had the creative disposition which his child acquired. Julia resembled her

mom who had passed on two years before her significant other. Mrs. Barnes had been unoriginal and skilled. It was a direct result of her that Julia had hitched a modeler, and was living in a cozy condo in Chicago, that Baldwin Junior had gone through school and had a few months at a craftsmanship school before the conflict came on, and that Jane, the most youthful, had a feeling of frugality, and a serious involvement with homegrown economy.
With respect to the remainder of her, Jane was twenty, thin as a Florentine page, and genuinely lovely. She was infatuated with life and jumped at the chance to discuss it. Youthful Baldwin said, to be sure, with the forthrightness of a sibling, that Jane ran on like a chattering creek.
She was "running on" this November morning, as she and youthful Baldwin had breakfast together. Jane generally got the morning meal. Sophy, a proficient negro lady, came over later to assist with the housework, and to put the six o'clock supper on the table. Yet, it was Jane who began the percolator, poached the eggs, and made the toast on the electric toaster oven, while youthful Baldwin read the Washington Post. He read bits without holding back when he was in that frame of mind. He was not generally in that frame of mind, and afterward Jane conversed with him. He didn't necessarily in every case tune in, however that had no effect.
Jane had named the percolator "Philomel," due to its purling harmonies.

"Don't you cherish it, Baldy?"
Her sibling, with one eye on the paper, was eating his grapefruit.
"Love what?"
"Philomel."
"Senseless stuff — — "
"It isn't. I like to hear it sing."
"In my current state of mind I lean toward a psalm of disdain."
She buttered a cut of toast for him.
"Indeed, obviously, you'd feel like that."
"Who wouldn't?" He took the toast from her, and covered himself in his paper, so Jane buttered one more cut for her and ate it in fighting quietness — in addition to a poached egg, and some espresso rich with yellow cream and much sugar. Jane's slenderness made such guilty pleasure conceivable. She delighted in great food as she partook in another gown, violets in the spring, the vista from the west front of the Capitol, free stanza, and the book of Job. There were actually no restrictions to Jane's enthusiasm. She talked again of the percolator. "It's basically as decent as a pot on the hob, right?"
Youthful Baldwin read on.
"I essentially love breakfast," she proceeded.
"Is there anything you don't cherish, Janey?" with a dash of disturbance.
"Indeed."
"What?"
"You."
He gazed at her over the sheet.
"That's what I like!"
"Indeed, you won't converse with me, Baldy. It isn't my issue assuming you can't stand the world."

"No, it isn't." He set out the paper. "Yet, I'll let you know this, Janey, I'm about through."
She paused to rest, then flung out, "Goodness, you're not. Be a decent game, Baldy. Things will undoubtedly come your direction assuming you stand by."
He gave a short snicker and rose. "I wish I had your good faith."
"I wish you had."
They confronted one another, searching for the second rather like two youthful cockerels. Jane's weaved hair underlined the innocent impact of her straight, thin figure. Baldy overshadowed her, his dark hair matching hers, his eyes, as well, coordinating — dim and illuminated. Jane was quick to dismiss her eyes. She checked the call every day.
"You'll be late."
He got his cap and coat and returned to her. "I'm an accused sorehead. Give me a kiss, Janey."
She gave it to him, and stuck to him briefly. "Remember to bring a steak home for supper," was all she said, yet he knew about the stroke of those gripping fingers.
It was one of his complaints that he needed to do the promoting — one couldn't rely upon Sherwood's single little store — so Baldy with dreams in his mind drove two times every week to the butcher's slow down in the old Center Market to bring back cleaves, or a porterhouse, or a merry little dish. He lacked the capacity to deal with it in the mornings, be that as it may. His little Ford took him over the back roads and through the city roads and

landed him at the Patent Office at a fourth of nine. There, with a half hour for lunch, he worked until five — it was a wretched existence and he had different yearnings.

Jane, left to herself, read the paper. One title was electrifying. The lady of a trendy wedding had been abandoned at the raised area. The groom had neglected to show up at the congregation. The visitors standing by anxiously in the seats had been educated, at last, that the function would be deferred.

Paper men chasing after the groom discovered that he had left a note for his best man — and that he was en route to southern waters. The lady of the hour remained invisible. Her uncle, who was likewise her watchman, and with whom she lived, had expressed that all in all nothing remained to be said. That was all. Yet, society was stealthily. Delafield Simms was the child of a rich New Yorker. He and his lady of the hour were to have spent their special night on his yacht. Edith Towne had a fortune to match his. The two of them had a place with old and privileged families. No big surprise individuals were talking.

There was an image of Miss Towne, a tall, fair young lady, in genuine ribbon, orange blooms, seed pearls — — . Pride was in each line of her. Jane's delicate extravagant conveyed her to that first short of breath second when the lady had worn that generous outfit and had studied herself in the mirror. "How cheerful she probably was." Then the last shivering fiasco.

Sophy showed up right away, and Jane educated her. "She won't ever dare trust anyone, will she?"
Sophy was savvy, and she gauged the inquiry out of her wide experience of human instinct. She was unable to pursue or compose, and she was subject to everyone around her for everyday announcements of the manner in which the enormous world went. Yet, she had worked in numerous families and had her very own group. So she knew life, which is something greater now and again than books.
"Yo' kain't at any point tell what a lady will do, Miss Janey. Effen she a trusting' nature, she'll trust' and trust', and effen she ain' a trustin' nature, she won't trust' nohow."
"However, what do you guess caused him to make it happen?"
"No one knows what a man's wife does, when it comes to gittin' wedded."
"In any case, to leave her like that, Sophy. I ought to think she'd bite the dust."
"Effen the great Lord let ladies kick the bucket when men 'received them," Sophy declared with a laugh, "dere wouldn't' be a female led' when the trump sounded." Her plate was heaped high with dishes, as she remained in the lounge area entryway. "Does all of you need rice pudding' fo' dinner, Miss Janey?"
Also, there the subject dropped. However, Jane considered an incredible arrangement if it happened with her work.

She told her sister, Julia, about it when, late that evening, she thought of her week after week letter.

"The most awful of it probably was to lose her confidence in things. I'd prefer to be Jane Barnes with no relationship than Edith Towne with a relationship like that. Baldy let me know a few days ago that I am not ugly! Might you at any point see him saying it? Furthermore, he doesn't think I'm pretty. Maybe I'm not. Yet, there are minutes, Judy, when I such as myself — — !

"Baldy almost threw a tantrum when I bounced my hair. In any case, I did it and faced the results, and it's no closure agreeable. Baldy right now is mid-Victorian. It is his response from the conflict. He says he is dead tired of flappers. That they are indistinguishable — and make no enticement for the creative mind! He returned home a few evenings ago from a dance and read Tennyson — could you at any point fancy that after the manner in which he used to excursion Amy Lowell at us and Carl Sandburg? He says he is so burnt out on short skirts and knees and propositions and cigarettes that he will chase with a weapon, assuming that he at any point chooses to wed, for an Elaine or a Griselda! In any case, the most exceedingly terrible of it is, he takes it out on me! I wish you'd see the manner in which he controls my garments and my habits, and I stay here like a detainee in a pinnacle while focusing on not a man but rather Evans Follette, and he is only a grief, Judy.

"Baldy has had three propositions; he said that the first was invigorating, however redundancy 'staled the interest'! Obviously he didn't let me know the names of the young ladies. Baldy's not a lowlife.
"In any case, he is deterred and frantically discouraged. He has such a major ability, Judy, and he simply works really hard at that old office. He expresses that after those years in France, it appears to be an enclosure. Some of the time I can't help thinking about what human advancement is, at any rate, that we cut the wings of our young hawks. We take our young men and shut them up, and they gasp for opportunity. Is that all that life will mean for Baldy — eight hours per day — in jail?
"However I am attempting to keep him at it until the house is paid for. I don't know whether I am correct — however it's all we have — and the two of us love it. He hasn't been capable of late to work much around evening time, he's dead drained. In any case, there's an award proposition of a magazine cover plan, and I maintain that he should contend. He says there isn't any utilization of his attempting to do anything except if he can give all of his opportunity to it.
"Obviously you've heard this previously, however I hear it consistently. Furthermore, I like to work things out. I should not compose a different line, dearest. Also, you can definitely relax, Baldy will work like distraught assuming the state of mind strikes him.

"Did I let you know that Evans Follette and his mom are to feast with us on Thanksgiving Day? We should have six visitors to make things go. However, no one will find a place with the Follettes. You know why, so I shouldn't for even a moment need to make sense of it.

"Kiss both of the children for me. Bombing other youthful things, I will have a Christmas tree for the cat. It's a gay life, dear.

"Ever your own,

"Jane."

The murkiness had stopped when she had completed her letter. She changed her gown for a more slender one, enveloped herself by an old cape of orange-shaded material, and went out to secure her chickens. She had taken care of them before she thought of her letter, yet she generally investigated to be certain they were protected.

She went through the still kitchen, where old Sophy sat by the warm, splendid reach. There were potatoes heating up, and Sophy's well known pudding. "How great everything smells," said Jane.

She grinned at Sophy and went on. The breeze was blowing and the sky was clear. There had been no snow, however there were little pools of ice about, and Jane took every one with a slide. She felt a shivering feeling of youth and excitement. Back of the carport was a shadowy woods of tall pines which sang and moaned as the breeze cleared them. There was a youthful moon over the pines. Jane couldn't help suspecting that her spirit was lifted to it. She flung up her arms to the moon, and the yellow cape surged about her.

The shed where the chickens were kept was back of the carport. At the point when Jane opened the entryway, her old Persian feline, Merrymaid, emerged to her, and a puff-chunk of a cat. Jane snapped on the lights in the chicken-house and the biddies mixed. At the point when she snapped them off once more, she heard them settle back to protected sleep.

The little cat moved in front of her, and the old feline moved as well, as the breeze spun her extraordinary tail about. "We won't go in the house — we won't go in the house," said Jane, in a kind of conversational serenade, as the pussies followed her down a way which drove through the pines. She frequently strolled at this hour — and she cherished it best on evenings like this.

She felt powerfully the excellence of it — the dull pines and the little moon above them — the pull of the breeze at her shroud like a wild close friend. Baldy was by all accounts not the only writer in the family, however Jane's adoration for excellence was garbled. She could always be unable to get it written down or draw it with a pencil. Down the way she went, the two felines like little shadows afterward, until unexpectedly a voice emerged from the dim.

"I accept it is little Jane Barnes."

She halted. "Goodness, is that you, Evans? Isn't it a sublime evening?"

"I don't know."

"Try not to talk that way."

"What difference would it make?"
"Since a night like this is like wine — it goes to my head."
"You are like wine," he told her. "Jane, how would you make it happen?"
"Do what?"
"Hold the posture of youth and delight and bliss?"
"You realize it's anything but a posture. I simply feel as such, Evans."
"My dear, I accept what you do."
He limped a little as he strolled close to her. He was tall and skinny. Bizarrely tall. However when he had done battle he had not appeared to be at all unusual. He had been tall yet not slight, and he had gone in all the magnificence of his awesome youth. There was no magnificence left. He was 27. He had battled and he would battle again for a similar reason. Yet, his childhood was dead, aside from when he was with Jane. She resuscitated him, as he said, similar to wine.
"I was coming over," he started, and a sibilant sound hindered him.
"Goodness, are the felines with you? Indeed, Rusty should accept the street," he snickered as the little old canine jogged to nonpartisan ground at the edge of the forest. Corroded was companions with Merrymaid, aside from when there were little cats about. He knew to the point of staying away from her in long periods of restless parenthood.
Jane got the cat. "They will come."
"All creatures follow you. You're somewhat of a homegrown Circe — with your canines and chickens and

felines in the spot of tigers and lions and panthers."

"I'd very much want to have lived in Eden," said Jane, suddenly, "before Eve and Adam trespassed. What it probably intended to have is that large number of incredible monsters unassuming and murmuring under your hand like this cat. Something unpleasant occurred, Evans, when dread appeared on the scene."

"What compels you to say that now, Jane?" His voice was sharp.

"Shouldn't I have said it? Gracious, Evans, you can't think I had you as a top priority — — "

"No," with a hint of exhaustion, "however you are the one to focus on, truly, who can say for sure what a defeatist I am — — "

"Evans, you're not."

"You're great to say it, however that is the very thing that I came over for. I'm facing it once more, Jane. A few cousins are from New York — they're at the New Willard — and Mother and I went in to see them the previous evening. They have welcomed us to return with them. They have a major house east of Fifth Avenue, and they need us as their visitors endlessly. They figure it will significantly help me for sure — get me out of myself, they call it. However, I can't see it. Since I returned home — each time I consider confronting hordes of individuals" — again his voice developed sharp — "I'm grasped by something I can't portray. It is entirely nonsensical, however I can't resist."

Briefly they strolled peacefully, then, at that point, he continued — "Mother's exceptionally sharp about it. She figures it will set me up. In any case, I need to remain here — and I believe in the event that you'd converse with her, she'll pay attention to you, Jane — she generally does."

"Does she have any idea how you feel about it?"

"No, I don't think so. I've never told her. I've simply gushed out to you sometimes. It would hurt Mother, no closure, to realize how transformed I am."

Jane laid her hand on his arm. "You're not. Support up, old dear. You're not dead yet." As she lifted her head to gaze toward him, the hood of her cape slipped back, and the breeze blew her delicate, thick hair against his cheek. "Yet, I'll converse with your mom on the off chance that you need me to. She is an extraordinary sweetheart."

Jane intended what she said; she was actually quite enamored with Mrs. Follette. What's more, in this she was not normal for the remainder of the society in Sherwood. Mrs. Follette was very disliked in the Park.

They had arrived at the kitchen entryway. "Won't you come in?" Jane said.

"No, I must get back. I just ran over briefly. I must have a day to day taste of you, Jane."

"Baldy's bringing a steak for supper. Assist us with eating it."

"Unfortunately Mother would be separated from everyone else."

"When will I converse with her?"

"There's no rush. The cousins are remaining on for the kickoff of

Congress. Jane dear, don't detest me — — " His voice broke.
"Evans, as though I could."
Again her hand was on his arm. He laid his own over it. "You're really amazing ever, Janey," he said, huskily — and as of now he disappeared.
Jane, going in, found that Baldy had called. "He ain't got here until seven," Sophy told her.
"You would be advised to run home," Jane told her. "I'll cook the steak when it comes."
Sophy was old and she was worn out. Life hadn't been simple. The child who was to have been the prop of her advanced age had been killed in France. There was a little girl who had gone north and who sometimes sent cash. Old Sophy didn't have any idea where her granddaughter got the cash, yet having it when it came was great. In any case, it was not, so old Sophy worked.
"I prefer not to let you be here, Miss Janey."
"Goodness, run along, Sophy. Baldy will precede I know it."
So Sophy went and Jane paused. Seven o'clock showed up, with the supper giving indications of disintegration. Jane sat at the front window and watched. The old feline watched, as well, roosted on the ledge, and looked out into the dull with round, strange eyes. The little cat dozed on the hearth. Jane became fretful and stood up, looking out. Then at the same time two round moons emerged over the skyline, were lost as the street plunged down, showed again on the ascent of the slope, and

lit the grass as Baldy's vehicle made a half circle and cleared into the carport. Jane passed through the kitchen to the secondary passage, tossing an assessing look at the things in the warming broiler, and stood looking out for the limit, embracing herself in the perception of the breeze.

As of now her sibling's tall structure was outlined against the shiny dim of the evening.

"I thought you were rarely coming," she told him.

"I suspected as much, as well." He bowed and kissed her; his cheek was cold as it contacted hers.

"Might it be said that you are almost frozen?"

"No. I sincerely apologize for being late, honey. Eat on the table and I'll be prepared — — "

"I'm apprehensive things will not be extremely tempting," she told him; "they've stood by so long. Yet, I'll cook the steak — — "

He had gone on, and was past her voice. She opened the fat bundle which he had saved on the kitchen table. She pondered a piece at its size. However, Baldy had an approach to bringing back surprising deals — twelve boxes of wafers — inconvenient pounds of espresso. However, this was neither wafers nor espresso. The container which was uncovered dragged the name of a stylish flower specialist. Inside were violets — single ones — set off by one wonderful rose and attached with a silver lace.

Jane wheezed — then, at that point, she went to the entryway and called:

"Baldy, where's the steak?"
He came to the highest point of the steps. "Extraordinary firearms," he said, "I failed to remember them!" Then he saw the violets in her grasp, giggled and descended a stage or two. "I sold a portion of bread and purchased — white hyacinths — — "
"They're radiant!" Her look cleared depending upon him. "Olive branch?"
There were gay flashes in his eyes. "We'll call it that."
She made a gesture of blowing a kiss to him from the tips of her fingers. "They are totally sweet. Furthermore, we can have an omelet. Provided that we eat additional eggs, we'll fold our wings."
"It doesn't matter at all to me what we have. I am so eager to eat at home."
He returned up the steps, giggling.
Jane, breaking eggs into a bowl, mulled over the casualness of men. She contemplated, as well, on the secret of Baldy's temperament. The blossoms were proof of high magnification. He didn't frequently loan himself to such luxury.
He descended by and by and helped convey the late supper. The potatoes lay like wilted leaves in a silver dish, the cornbread was a crumpled wreck, the pudding a crime. Just Jane's omelet and a lettuce salad had gotten away from the curse of postponement. Then, at that point there was Philomel, singing. Jane drew some espresso, hot and solid, and set it at her sibling's place. The violets were in the focal point of the table, the felines murmuring on the hearth.

Jane cherished her little home with practically energetic power. Yet again she wanted to have Baldy in a state of mind like this — things right with his reality.

She realized it was so by the ring of his voice, the rooster of his head — thus she was not at all shocked when he inclined forward under the dated spreading vault which doused him with light, and said, "I've such a great deal to tell you, Jane; the most astonishing thing has occurred."

## Part II

## A PRINCESS PASSES

Whenever youthful Baldwin Barnes had braved Sherwood that morning while heading to Washington, his vehicle had cleared by fields which were fresh and frozen; by clusters of trees whose sharp tops cut into the unmistakable blue of the sky; over ice-bound streams, all sparkling silver in the early daylight.

It was freezing, and his little vehicle was available to the climate. Yet, he felt no chill. He wore the mustard-hued top-coat which had been his lieutenant's attire in the military. The collar was gone up to safeguard his ears. His face showed pink and wedge-molded between his delicate cap and his collar.

He had the eye of a craftsman, and he enjoyed the ride. Indeed, even in winter the field was appealing — and as the street got away, there came a couple of large houses encompassed by wide grounds, with looks through their high supports of white sculptures, of spired cedars, of sun-dials set amidst dead gardens.

Past these there was a dry stretch until the Lake was reached, then the connections of one nation club, the old structures of another, and finally on the peak of a slope, a perspective on the city — clearing on the right towards Arlington and on the left towards Soldiers' Home.
Moving toward Sixteenth Street, he crossed an extension with its supports protected by stone jaguars — and it was on this scaffold that his vehicle halted.
Moving out, he accused Fate irately. Years a while later, be that as it may, he tried not consider the distinction it could have made on the off chance that his little flivver had not bombed him.
He raised the hood and tapped and fiddled. Once in a while he stopped to stamp his feet or beat his hands together. Also, he expressed things softly. He would be late at the workplace — life was only one — darned thing — after another!
Once when he halted, a lady passed him. She was tall and slim and enveloped dependent upon her ears by moleskin. Her little cap was blue, from her hand swung a dim softened cowhide sack, her feet were in dark shoes with cut-steel clasps.
Baldy's fast eyes took in the subtleties of her ensemble. He reflected as he returned to work that ladies were boneheads to court passing in that style, with flimsy shoes and silk stockings, in this harsh climate.
He tracked down the difficulty, fixed it, bounced into his vehicle and turned over his engine. What's more, it was

similar as he was moving that his eye was spotted by a spot of blue swaying down the slope beneath the extension. The one who had passed him was advancing gradually along the tricky way. On each side of her the trees were brown and exposed. At the foot of the slope was a string of frozen water.

It was not regular right now to see walkers there. Every so often a worker pursued a faster route — or on warm days there were cookout parties — yet to follow the unpleasant ways in winter was a grim and strenuous experience. He remained briefly to watch her, then, at that point, abruptly left his vehicle and ran. The young lady in the blue cap had gotten her high heels in a root, had staggered and fallen.

At the point when he contacted her, she was battling to her feet. He helped her, and got the sack which she had dropped.

"Many thanks." Her voice was low and satisfying. He saw that she was youthful, that her skin was extremely fair, and that the hair which cleared over her ears was pale gold, yet in particular, he saw that her eyes were consuming blue. He had never seen eyes very like them. The old writers would have called them sapphire, yet sapphires don't fire.

"It was so senseless of me to attempt to make it happen," she was dissenting, "however I figured it very well may be an easy route — — "

He thought about what her objective may be that this distant way ought to prompt it. However, all he said was,

"High heels aren't made for — hiking — — "

"They aren't made for anything," she expressed, peering down at the steel-clasped shoes, "valuable."

"Allow me to help you up the slope."

"I would rather not go up."

He overviewed the lofty grade. "I'm entirely certain you would rather not go down."

"I do," she wavered, "yet I guess I can't."

He had an unexpected motivation. "Could I at any point take you anyplace? My little fiver is up there on the extension. Would you see any problems with that?"

"Would I see any problems if a day to day existence line were tossed to me in mid-sea?" She said it daintily, however he liked there was a note of high expectation.

They went up the slope together. "I need to get an Alexandria vehicle," she told him.

"Be that as it may, you are miles from it."

"Am I?" She showed a passing disarray. "I — trusted I could arrive at it through the Park — — "

"You may. Be that as it may, you could likewise stick to death in the endeavor like a darling in the woods, with next to no robins to play out the last despairing ceremonies. Made your thought process something like this?"

He saw without a moment's delay his error. Her voice had a dash of coldness. "I can't tell you."

"Sorry," he said unexpectedly. "You should excuse me."

She liquefied. "No, I ought to be pardoned. It should look abnormal to you — however I'd prefer not to — make sense of — — "

On the last steep ascent of the slope he lifted her over a dangerous pool, and as his hand sank into the delicate fur of her wrap, he was aware of its extravagance. He couldn't help suspecting that his mustard-hued coat genuinely yelled ambiguity. His creative mind cleared on to Raleigh, and the velvet shroud which could do what is going on equity. He grinned at himself and grinning, as well, at her, felt a shivering feeling of the coming situation.

It was a direct result of that grin, and its sincere, innocent nature, that she confided in him. "Do you know," she said, "I haven't had anything to eat earlier today, and I'm terribly eager. Is there any spot where I could have some espresso — where you could bring it out to me in the vehicle?"

"Could I?" the morning stars sang. "There's a stopping place in Georgetown."

"Without the world looking on?"

"Without your reality looking on," strongly.

She faltered, then came clean. "I'm taking off — — "

He was enthusiastic. "May I help?"

"Maybe you wouldn't assume that you knew."

"Attempt me."

He helped her into his vehicle, tucked the carpet about her, and set up the shades. "Nobody can see you on the rearward sitting arrangement," he

said, and headed to Georgetown on the wings of the breeze.
He brought espresso out to her from a slick shop where milk was sold, and buns, and hot beverages, to motormen and guides. It was a perfect little spot, new as paint, and the buttered rolls were brown and fresh.
"I tasted nothing so great," the out of control told Baldy. "Furthermore, presently I will request that you drive me over the Virginia side — I'll get the streetcar there."
When finally he drew up at a little way station, and detached the drape, he knew that she had opened the softened cowhide sack and had a roll of bills in her grasp. Briefly his heart bombed him. Is it true or not that she planned to offer him cash?
In any case, what she said, with cheeks blazing, was: "I haven't anything short of ten bucks. Do you figure they will take it?"
"It's far-fetched. I have tons of progress." He held out a modest bunch of silver.
"Many thanks, and — you should allow me to have your card — — "
"Good gracious — — "
Her voice had an edge of sharpness. "Obviously it should be a credit."
He gave her his card peacefully. She read the name. "Mr. Barnes, you have been exceptionally kind. I'm hugely appreciative."
"It was not benevolence — yet once in a while a princess passes."
Briefly her stunned look met his — then the clank of a chime proclaimed a coming vehicle.

As he helped her out quickly she staggered over the mat. He got her up, lifted her to the ground, and motioned to the motorman.

The vehicle halted and she mounted the means. "Farewell, and many thanks." He remained back and she waved to him while he watched her concealed.

His work at the workplace that morning had dreams for a backup. He went out at noon but didn't eat anything. It was at noon that he purchased the violets — following through on an unfathomable cost for them, and not mindful.

He had wild considerations of following the way to Alexandria — of tracking down his Juliet in a few galleries and scaling to her. Or on the other hand of sending the roses forward addressed generally to "a One "A Princess passed." One proved unable, in any case, to make certain of an uncomprehending mail administration. He would require more clear sobriquet.

He had not, to be sure, purchased the blossoms for Jane. He had not considered his sister and he passed the flower vendor's window. He had been brought into the shop by the relationship of thoughts — when he entered all the fragrance and pleasantness appeared to have a place with a nursery wherein his woman strolled.

He had no lunch, and he took the container of violets back with him to the workplace, wrapped to enormous size to safeguard it from the virus. It was an object of much interest to his individual representatives as it sat on the window-ledge. They generally needed to know who it was for, and one of the loathed flappers, who, on occasion, took Baldy's correspondence, attempted to peep between the covers.

He felt that her look would be defilement. What did she know about fragile aromas? Her fragrances were oriental, and she utilized lipstick!

He made due, nonetheless, to cart the thing away softly. He was, according to the workplace, a gay and friendly chap. They remained unaware of his responses. Also, he was famous.

So presently he told the young lady, "Assuming that you'll leave that be, I'll bring a container of chocolates for the group."

"For what reason mightn't I at any point check it out?"

"Since interest is a dangerous sin. You realize what has been going on with Bluebeard's better half?"

"Gracious, Bluebeard." She had pursued him, she thought, in the Paris papers. He had killed a ton of spouses. She chuckled a little in regard to the fierceness of the subject. Then nailed him down to his commitment of desserts. "You realize the benevolent we like?"

"This week?"

"Indeed. Margarine creams."

"Last week it was the nut kind. One won't ever be aware. I ought to figure you should normalize your preferences."

"That could be inept, couldn't it? It's considerably more energizing to change."

He returned to his work and failed to remember her. She was one of the butterflies who had fluttered to Washington during the conflict, and had set that moderate city by the ears in disobedience of custom.
It was these young ladies who had eaten their snacks inside the holy regions of Lafayette Square, hanging themselves on its sculptures at early afternoon, and flinging its flawless sod with broken boxes and packs, who had worn sheer and inadequate dress, had motored under the moon and without a moon, unchaperoned, until morning, and had come through everything somewhat harmed, maybe, as to beliefs, however having made an unequivocal dazzle on the existence of the capital. The cavern occupants were dead. For better, for more terrible, the conflict specialist and the ladies of old Washington had been cleared out together from a protected and cozy harbor into the seething oceans of social rearrangement.
It was after office that Baldy conveyed the blossoms to his vehicle. He set the crate on the secondary lounge. In the rush of the morning he had failed to remember the mat which actually lay where his fair traveler had staggered over it. He got it and something dropped from its folds. It was the dim softened cowhide sack, half open, and showing the roll of bills. Underneath the roll of bills was a little sheer tissue, a vanity case with a spot of powder and a small puff, another check-book — and, carelessly at the extremely base, a ring — a ring of such charm that as it lay in Baldy's grasp, he

questioned its existence. The band was of platinum, thin, yet sufficiently able to endure a cut moonstone surrounded by precious stones. The cutting showed a fragile Psyche — with a butterfly on her shoulder. The precious stones blasted like little suns. Inside the ring was an engraving — "Del to Edith — Forever."

Del to Edith? Where had he seen those names? With an unexpected blaze of brightening, he dropped the ring once more into the sack, stuffed the pack in his pocket, and advanced toward a newsy corner.

There it was in surprising titles: Edith Towne Disappears. Delafield Simms' Yacht Said to Have Been Sighted Near Norfolk!

So his traveler had been the much-discussed Edith Towne — abandoned right now of her marriage!

He thought about her eyes consuming blue, — the reasonableness of her skin and hair — the hint of haughtiness. Simms was a mutt, obviously! He ought to have bowed at her feet!

What to do was to return the sack once again to her. He should publicize without a moment's delay. On the wings of this choice, his vehicle spun down the Avenue. The lines which, after much pondering, he pushed across the counter of the paper office, would be equivalent to other people, yet obvious to her. "Will a traveler who left a sack with significant items in a Ford vehicle hit up Sherwood Park 49."

Part III

JANE KNITS

"Is she truly that wonderful?" Jane requested.
"What?"
"Her image in the paper."
"Haven't I expressed enough for you to know it?"
Jane gestured. "Indeed. Be that as it may, it doesn't sound genuine to me. Is it true or not that you are certain you didn't dream it?"
"I'll say I didn't. Isn't that confirmation?" The dark pack lay on the table before them, the ring was on Jane's finger.
She went to get the light. "Baldy," she expressed, "it's past creative mind."
"I told you — — "
"Consider having a ring like this — — "
"Think," savagely, "of having a sweetheart who took off."
"Well," said Jane, "a few benefits are being — unsought. I'm similar to the Miller-ess of Dee —
"I care for no one —
Actually no, not I,
Since no one
Cares —
For me — — !"
She sang it with a light innocent swing of her body. Her voice was silly and sweet, with a bit of imposingness.
Baldy flung his disdain at her. "Jane, would you confirm or deny that you are ever vigorous?"
"Irregularly," she grinned at him, came over and wrapped her arm up his. "Baldy," she cajoled, "would you confirm or deny that you will tell her uncle?"
He gazed at her. "Her uncle? Let him know what?"

"That you've tracked down the pack." He flung off her arm. "Could you have me turn swindler?"
"Sky, Baldy, this isn't acting. It's not unexpected. You can't keep that sack."
"I can keep it until she answers my ad."
"She might in all likelihood never see your ad, and the cash isn't yours, and the ring isn't."
He was in pain. "Yet, she confided in me. I can't make it happen."
Jane shrugged her shoulders, and started to gather up the supper things. Baldy helped her. Old Merrymaid mewed to go out, and Jane opened the entryway.
"It's snowing hard," she said.
The breeze drove the chips across the limit. Old Merrymaid moved once more into the house, excited and round as a muff. The air was freezing.
"It will be a loathsome evening," Baldwin, weighty with despair, forecasted. He considered Edith, in the tempest in her clasped shoes. Had she tracked down the cover? Is it safe to say that she was scared and alone in some place in obscurity?
He went into the front room, whence Jane followed him. Jane was weaving a sweater and she worked while Baldy read to her. He read the full record of Edith Towne's flight. She had disappeared promptly toward the beginning of the day. The housekeeper, taking her morning meal dependent upon her, had found the room vacant. She had left a note for her uncle. In any case, he had not

allowed its distribution. He was, they expressed, wild with tension.

"I'll wager he's an old dictator," was Baldy's remark.

Frederick Towne's image was in the paper. "I like his face," said Jane, "and he doesn't appear to be so unpleasantly old."

"For what reason would it be a good idea for her to take off from him, in the event that he wasn't a dictator?" he requested irately.

"Indeed, don't chide me." Jane was pretty much as distinctive as an oriole amidst her orange fleeces.

She cherished variety. The family room was an outflow of it. Its furniture was dated however not outdated enough to be exquisite. Jane had, nonetheless, changed its absence of beauty and its dull monotonous fronts of chintz — tropical birds against high contrast stripes — and there was a light of dull blue ceramics with a Chinese shade. A fire in the coal grind, with the sparkle of the light, provided the room with a look of polished brilliance. The little cat, nestled into Jane's lap, played comfortably with the brownish strings.

"Try not to chasten me," said Jane, "it isn't my issue."

"I'm not reproving, however I'm concerned about death. What's more, you're not any assistance, right?"

She checked out at him in amazement. "I've attempted to help. I advised you to call up."

Youthful Baldwin strolled the floor.

"She confided in me."

"You will not go anywhere with that," expressed Jane with choice. "What to do is to tell Mr. Towne that you have fresh insight about her, and that you'll just remain conservative that he will do nothing until he has talked it over with you."

"That sounds better," said youthful Baldwin; "how could you end up considering it?"

"Sometimes," said Jane, "I have thoughts."

Baldy went to the phone. At the point when he returned his eyes resembled dark moons. "He guaranteed everything, and he's emerging — — "

"Here?"

"Indeed, he wouldn't hold on until to-morrow. He's crazy about her — — "

"Indeed, he would be." Jane intellectually overviewed the circumstance. "Baldy, I will make some espresso, and have some cheddar and saltines."

"He may not need them."

"On a chilly night like this, I'll say he will; anyone would."

Baldy assisted Jane with getting out the round-bellied silver pot, the pitchers and plate. The youngsters had a feeling of lack of concern as they took care of the old silver. Frederick Towne might not have anything of more recognized history. It had a place with their incredible grandma, Dabney, who was truly D'Aubigne, and it had graced an Emperor's table. Each piece had a monogram set in an engraved wreath. The enormous plate was weighty to the point that Jane lifted it with trouble, so Badly set it for her on the little mahogany table which they drew up before the fire. There was no

abundance now in the Barnes family, however the old silver discussed when a youthful leader as dark haired as Jane had apportioned rich cordiality. Frederick Towne had not expected what he found — the little house set high on its patios appeared to give from its brilliant lit window squares a welcome in obscurity. "I shan't be long, Briggs," he told his escort.
"Excellent, sir," said Briggs, and drove the way up the patio.
Baldy guided Towne into the lounge room, and Frederick, remaining on the limit, reviewed a comfort which helped him to not remember anything even a variety representation in some early English magazine. There was the coal grind, the table attracted to the fire, the shimmering silver on its enormous plate, violets in a low container — and ascending to meet him, a slim, gleaming youngster, with a flag of orange fleece behind her.
"Jane," said youthful Barnes, "may I present Mr. Towne?" and Jane held out her hand and said, "This is awesome of you."
He thought of himself as startlingly charitable. He was not charitable 100% of the time. He had felt that he was unable to be. A man with cash and position needed to quiet himself down once in a while in a shell of save, in case he was forced upon. Be that as it may, in this glow and scent he extended. "What an enchanting room," he said, and grinned at her.
Her most memorable perspective on him affirmed the assessment she framed from his image. He was

evidently not north of forty, a stocky, very much constructed, reddish man, with fair hair that waved freshly, and with clear blue eyes, lighter, she advanced subsequently, than Edith's, yet with simply a touch of that consuming blue. He had the quality of indefinable completion which discusses a daily existence spent in the right school and the right school, and the right clubs, of a foundation of ages of good blood and great reproduction. He wore evening garments, and one knew some way or another that supper never tracked him down without them.

However, disregarding these confirmations of fanfare, Jane felt flawlessly quiet with him. He was, all things considered, she reflected, just a noble man, and that's what baldy was. The main distinction lay in their dissimilar salaries. In this way, as the two men talked, she weaved on, with the outward impact of placidity.

"Do you believe that I should go?" she had asked them, and Towne had answered expeditiously, "Surely not. There's nothing we need to say that you can't hear."

So Jane tuned in with every one of her ears, and adjusted the assessment she had shaped of Frederick Towne from his image and from her most memorable look at him. He was good to converse with, however he may be hard to live with. He had tenacity and narcissism.

"Why Edith ought to have gotten it done astounds me."

Jane, shrewdly recalling the Admiral's melody from Pinafore which had been her dad's #1, found it beating in her mind — My wonder, my shock, you might gain from the outflow of my eyes — —

Be that as it may, no touch of this displayed in her way.
"She was harmed," she said, "and she needed to stow away."
"In any case, individuals assume that here and there it is my shortcoming. I could do without that. It is unreasonable. We've forever been awesome companions — more like siblings than niece and uncle."
"Be that as it is, dislike Baldy and me," expressed Jane to herself, "not at all like Baldy and me."
"Obviously Simms should be shot," Towne told them heatedly.
"He should be hanged," was Baldy's correction.
Jane's needles clicked, yet she didn't say anything. She was biting the dust to let these savage guys know her thought process. How great could it shoot Delafield Simms? A lady's harmed pride isn't to be mended by the possibility of a man's dead body.
Youthful Baldwin drew out the sack. "It is one that Delafield gave her," Frederick expressed, "and I changed out a check for her at the bank the day preceding the wedding. I can't envision the reason why she took the ring with her."
"She presumably neglected to take it off; her psyche wasn't on rings."
Jane's voice was warm with feeling.
He checked out at her with some interest. "What was it on?"
"Gracious, her heart was broken. Nothing else really had any

significance. Mightn't you at any point see?"
He delayed the slightest bit before he talked. "I don't completely accept that it was broken. I scarcely think she adored him."
Baldy blasted, "Yet for what reason would it be a good idea for her to wed him?"
"Gracious, indeed, it was a decent match. An excellent match. Also, Edith's not at all profound — — "
"Truly?" said Jane wonderfully.
Baldy was quiet. Was Frederick Towne incognizant in regards to the marvels that lay behind those eyes of consuming blue?
Jane cleared them back to the issue of the sack. "We figured you should have it, Mr. Towne, yet Baldy had second thoughts about uncovering anything he realizes about Miss Towne's stowing away spot. He feels that she confided in him."
"You said you had been promoted, Mr. Barnes?"
"Indeed."
"Indeed, the one thing is to get her home. Let her know if she hits you up." Frederick looked abruptly worn out and old.
Baldy, resting up against the shelf, looked down at him. "It's difficult to conclude what I should do. Yet, I feel that I'm right in giving her an opportunity first to answer the ad."
Towne's tone showed a hint of disturbance. "Obviously you'll need to go about as you naturally suspect best."
"Mr. Towne, I will make you some espresso."

"I will be extremely appreciative," he grinned at her. What a beguiling youngster she was! He was mitigated and revived by the climate they made. This kid and young lady were a cordial pair and he cherished his straightforwardness. His own home, since Edith's takeoff, had been melancholy, and his companions had been split in their title among himself and Edith. Yet, the youthful Barneses were so wonderfully responsive with their illuminated eyes and their little demeanor of making him one with them. Edith had consistently appeared to put him most certainly on the rack. With little Jane and her sibling he had a sensation of balance old enough.
"Look here," he said rashly, "may I fill you in regarding it? It would ease my monstrous problems."
To Jane it was a completely exhilarating second. Having poured the espresso, she emerged from behind her bastion of silver and sat in her chintz seat. She didn't weave; she was captivated by the story that Towne was telling. She stood by, her hands collapsed, the tropical birds about her. To Frederick she appeared to be a bird herself — thin and wonderful, and with a voice that sang! Towne was not a susceptible man. His long stretches of bachelorhood had solidified him to ladylike expressions. Be that as it may, here was no slyness. Jane didn't accept anything. She was herself. As he conversed with her, he became mindful of some blended inclination. A practically young enthusiasm to sparkle as the legend of his story. In the event that

he weaved the subject, it was for her advantage. Everything he said was from his perspective. In any case, everything that he said was not reality, nor even 50% of it.

Section III

JANE KNITS

"Is she truly that lovely?" Jane requested.

"What?"

"Her image in the paper."

"Haven't I expressed enough for you to know it?"

Jane gestured. "Indeed. Be that as it may, it doesn't sound genuine to me. Could it be said that you are certain you didn't dream it?"

"I'll say I didn't. Isn't the evidence unreasonable?" The dark pack lay on the table before them, the ring was on Jane's finger.

She went to get the light. "Baldy," she expressed, "it's past creative mind."

"I told you — — "

"Consider having a ring like this — — "

"Think," furiously, "of having a darling who took off."

"Well," said Jane, "a few benefits are being — unsought. I'm similar to the Miller-ess of Dee —

"I care for no one —
Actually no, not I,
Since no one
Cares —
For me — — !"

She sang it with a light innocent swing of her body. Her voice was energetic and sweet, with a bit of imposingness. Baldy flung his contempt at her. "Jane, would you confirm or deny that you are ever decisive?"

"Irregularly," she grinned at him, came over and wrapped her arm up his.
"Baldy," she persuaded, "would you confirm or deny that you will tell her uncle?"
He gazed at her. "Her uncle? Let him know what?"
"That you've tracked down the pack."
He flung off her arm. "Could you have me turn backstabber?"
"Sky, Baldy, this isn't a drama. It's generally expected. You can't keep that sack."
"I can keep it until she answers my promotion."
"She might very well never see your notice, and the cash isn't yours, and the ring isn't."
He was upset. "Be that as it may, she confided in me. I can't make it happen."
Jane shrugged her shoulders, and started to clean up the supper things. Baldy helped her. Old Merrymaid mewed to go out, and Jane opened the entryway.
"It's snowing hard," she said.
The breeze drove the drops across the limit. Old Merrymaid moved once more into the house, excited and round as a muff. The air was freezing.
"It will be a ghastly evening," Baldwin, weighty with misery, forecasted. He considered Edith, in the tempest in her clasped shoes. Had she tracked down the cover? Is it safe to say that she was terrified and alone in some place in obscurity?
He went into the lounge, whence Jane as of now followed him. Jane was sewing a sweater and she worked while Baldy read to her. He read the

full record of Edith Towne's flight. She had disappeared promptly in the first part of the day. The house cleaner, taking her morning meal dependent upon her, had found the room unfilled. She had left a note for her uncle. However, he had not allowed its distribution. He was, they expressed, wild with uneasiness.

"I'll wager he's an old despot," was Baldy's remark.

Frederick Towne's image was in the paper. "I like his face," said Jane, "and he doesn't appear to be so unpleasantly old."

"For what reason would it be a good idea for her to take off from him, in the event that he wasn't a dictator?" he requested irately.

"All things considered, don't chide me." Jane was essentially as distinctive as an oriole amidst her orange fleeces.

She cherished variety. The lounge was a declaration of it. Its furniture was dated yet not outdated enough to be wonderful. Jane had, in any case, changed its absence of beauty and its dull monotonous fronts of chintz — tropical birds against high contrast stripes — and there was a light of dull blue stoneware with a Chinese shade. A fire in the coal grind, with the sparkle of the light, provided the room with a look of shined splendor. The little cat, nestled into Jane's lap, played comfortably with the brownish strings.

"Try not to chase me," said Jane, "it isn't my shortcoming."

"I'm not chiding, however I'm stressed to death. Also, you're not any assistance, right?"
She checked out at him in awe. "I've attempted to help. I advised you to call up."
Youthful Baldwin strolled the floor. "She confided in me."
"You will not go anywhere with that," expressed Jane with choice. "What to do is to tell Mr. Towne that you have fresh insight about her, and that you'll just provide a conservative estimate that he will do nothing until he has talked it over with you."
That sounds better," said youthful Baldwin; "how could you end up considering it?"
"Sometimes," said Jane, "I have thoughts."
Baldy went to the phone. At the point when he returned his eyes resembled dim moons. "He guaranteed everything, and he's emerging — — "
"Here?"
"Indeed, he wouldn't hold on until to-morrow. He's crazy about her — — "
"Indeed, he would be." Jane intellectually reviewed the circumstance. "Baldy, I will make some espresso, and have some cheddar and wafers."
"He may not need them."
"On a chilly night like this, I'll say he will; anyone would."
Baldy assisted Jane with getting out the round-bellied silver pot, the pitchers and plate. The youngsters had a feeling of lack of concern as they dealt with the old silver. Frederick Towne might not have anything of more recognized history. It had a

place with their extraordinary grandma, Dabney, who was truly D'Aubigne, and it had graced an Emperor's table. Each piece had a monogram set in an engraved wreath. The large plate was weighty to the point that Jane lifted it with trouble, so Badly set it for her on the little mahogany table which they drew up before the fire. There was no abundance now in the Barnes family, yet the old silver discussed when a youthful entertainer as dark haired as Jane had apportioned sumptuous neighborliness.

Frederick Towne had not expected what he found — the little house set high on its porches appeared to give from its brilliant lit window squares a welcome in obscurity. "I shan't be long, Briggs," he shared with his driver.

"Generally excellent, sir," said Briggs, and drove the way up the porch.

Baldy guided Towne into the family room, and Frederick, remaining on the limit, reviewed a comfort which helped him to not remember anything even a variety representation in some early English magazine. There was the coal grind, the table attracted to the fire, the shimmering silver on its monstrous plate, violets in a low container — and ascending to meet him, a thin, gleaming kid, with a pennant of orange fleece behind her.

"Jane," said youthful Barnes, "may I present Mr. Towne?" and Jane held out her hand and said, "This is awesome of you."

He thought of himself as startlingly benevolent. He was not thoughtful all of the time. He had felt that he was unable to be. A man with cash and position needed to quiet himself down in some cases in a shell of hold, in case he was forced upon.

In any case, in this glow and aroma he extended. "What a beguiling room," he said, and grinned at her.

Her most memorable perspective on him affirmed the assessment she framed from his image. He was evidently not north of forty, a stocky, very much fabricated, reddish man, with fair hair that waved freshly, and with clear blue eyes, lighter, she advanced a short time later than Edith's, yet with simply a touch of that consuming blue. He had the quality of indefinable completion which discusses a day to day existence spent in the right school and the right school, and the right clubs, of a foundation of ages of good blood and great rearing. He wore evening garments, and one knew some way or another that supper never tracked him down without them.

However despite these confirmations of fanfare, Jane felt flawlessly quiet with him. He was, all things considered, she reflected, just a refined man, and that's what baldy was. The main distinction lay in their unique wages. Thus, as the two men talked, she sewed on, with the outward impact of placidity.

"Do you maintain that I should go?" she had asked them, and Towne had answered speedily, "Absolutely not. There's nothing we need to say that you can't hear."

So Jane tuned in with every one of her ears, and changed the assessment she had shaped of Frederick Towne from his image and from her most memorable look at him. He was ideal to converse with, yet he may be hard to live with. He had persistence and retention.

"Why Edith ought to have gotten it done flabbergasts me."

Jane, wickedly recollecting the Admiral's tune from Pinafore which had been her dad's #1, found it beating in her mind — My shock, my amazement, you might gain from the statement of my eyes — —

In any case, no smidgen of this displayed in her way.

"She was harmed," she said, "and she needed to stow away."

"Yet, individuals generally assume that here and there it is my shortcoming. I could do without that. It is ridiculous. We've forever been awesome companions — more like siblings than niece and uncle."

"Be that as it is, dislike Baldy and me," expressed Jane to herself, "not at all like Baldy and me."

"Obviously Simms should be shot," Towne told them heatedly.

"He should be hanged," was Baldy's alteration.

Jane's needles clicked, however she didn't say anything. She was passing on to let these ruthless guys know her thought process. How great could it shoot Delafield Simms? A lady's harmed pride isn't to be mended by the prospect of a man's dead body. Youthful Baldwin drew out the sack. "It is one that Delafield gave her,"

Frederick expressed, "and I changed out a check for her at the bank the day preceding the wedding. I can't envision the reason why she took the ring with her."
"She most likely neglected to take it off; her brain wasn't on rings." Jane's voice was warm with feeling.
He checked out at her with some interest. "What was it on?"
"Goodness, her heart was broken. Nothing else really had any significance. Might you at any point see?"
He delayed the slightest bit before he talked. "I don't completely accept that it was broken. I scarcely think she cherished him."
Baldy blasted, "Yet for what reason would it be advisable for her to wed him?"
"Gracious, indeed, it was a decent match. An excellent match. What's more, Edith's not at all close to home — — "
"Truly?" said Jane agreeably.
Baldy was quiet. Was Frederick Towne oblivious in regards to the marvels that lay behind those eyes of consuming blue?
Jane cleared them back to the question of the pack. "We figured you should have it, Mr. Towne, however Baldy had doubts about uncovering anything he realizes about Miss Towne's stowing away spot. He feels that she confided in him."
"You said you had publicized, Mr. Barnes?"
"Indeed."
"Indeed, the one thing is to get her home. Let her know if she hits you

up." Frederick looked abruptly worn out and old.
Baldy, resting up against the shelf, looked down at him. "It's difficult to conclude what I should do. In any case, I feel that I'm right in giving her an opportunity first to answer the promotion."
Towne's tone showed a dash of disturbance. "Obviously you'll need to go about as you naturally suspect best."
"Mr. Towne, I will make you some espresso."
"I will be exceptionally appreciative," he grinned at her. What an enchanting youngster she was! He was alleviated and revived by the air they made. This kid and young lady were a well disposed pair and he cherished his simplicity. His own home, since Edith's flight, had been gloomy, and his companions had been split in their title among himself and Edith. In any case, the youthful Barneses were so charmingly responsive with their illuminated eyes and their little quality of making him one with them. Edith had consistently appeared to put him certainly on the rack. With little Jane and her sibling he had a sensation of equity old enough.
"Look here," he said rashly, "may I fill you in regarding it? It would ease my sight of any problems."
To Jane it was an exhilarating second. Having poured the espresso, she emerged from behind her bulwark of silver and sat in her chintz seat. She didn't sew; she was captivated by the story that Towne was telling. She stood by, her hands collapsed, the

tropical birds about her. To Frederick she appeared to be a bird herself — thin and wonderful, and with a voice that sang!

Towne was not a naive man. His long stretches of bachelorhood had solidified him to female expressions. In any case, there was no slyness. Jane didn't expect anything. She was herself. As he conversed with her, he became mindful of some blended inclination. A practically young enthusiasm to sparkle as the legend of his story. Assuming he weaved the subject, it was for her advantage. Everything that he said was from his perspective. Yet, everything that he said was not reality, nor even 50% of it.

## Part IV

## Excellence WAITS

Edith Towne had lived with her Uncle Frederick almost four years when she became drawn into Delafield Simms. Her mom was dead, similar to her dad. Frederick was her dad's just sibling, and had a major house to himself, after his mom's passing. It appeared to be the main shelter for his niece, so he asked her, and additionally asked his dad's cousin, Annabel Towne, to save the house for him, and chaperone Edith.

Annabel was north of sixty, and rather endless, however she effectively played respectability, and there was nothing else requested of her in Frederick's family of six workers. She was an evaporated and parched individual, with fixed thoughts of what one owed to society. Frederick's mom had been that way, so he wouldn't fret.

He fairly preferred to imagine that the lady of his family kept to old beliefs. It provided for things a quality of pride. Edith, when she came, was unique. So unique that Frederick was happy that she had three additional years at school before she would enjoy the winters with him. The summers were not hard to organize. Edith and Annabel concluded to the Towne bungalow on an island in Maine — and Frederick went up for week-closing and for the long stretch of August. Edith invested a lot of energy out-of-entryways with her young companions. She was somewhat attached to her Uncle Fred, however he didn't pose a potential threat not too far off from her young occupations. Then, at that point, came her colder time of year at home, and her ensuing commitment to Delafield Simms. It was a direct result of Uncle Fred that she became locked in. She essentially didn't have any desire to live with him any longer. She felt that Uncle Fred would absolutely love to have her go, and the inclination was shared. She was an elephant in his hands. Normally. He was an extraordinary old dear, yet he was a Turk. He didn't have any acquaintance with it, obviously. Yet, his thoughts of being an expert of his own home were entirely old fashioned. Cousin Annabel and the workers, and everyone in his office essentially held tight his words, and Edith wouldn't hang. She came into his unhitched male Paradise like a fairly inconvenient Eve, and requested her portion of the universe. He could have done without it, and you were right there.

It was truly Uncle Fred who believed that she should wed Delafield Simms. He discussed it a ton. At first Edith wouldn't tune in. In any case, Delafield was persevering and patient. He came steadily to be as a very remarkable piece of her regular day to day existence as the dinners she ate or the vehicle she drove. Uncle Fred was continuously welcoming him. He was perpetually available, and when he wasn't she missed him.

They felt for one another, she chose, the thing called "love." It was not, maybe, the sentiment which one tracked down in books. Yet, she had been educated cautiously at school to doubt sentiment. The accentuation had been laid on the transient nature of young adult inclination. One wedded for the race, and one picked, legitimately, with one's head all things being equal, as in the days of yore, with the heart.

So there you had it. Delafield was qualified. He was solid, possessed intellect enough, an OK code of ethics — and was able to allow her to have her own particular manner. In the event that there were minutes when Edith contemplated whether this program was satisfactory to married joy, she set the idea to the side. She and Delafield enjoyed each other's closure. Why stress?

What's more, truly on occasion Uncle Fred was incomprehensible. His mom had resided until he was 35, she had loved him, and had given to Cousin Annabel and to the old workers in the house the recipe by which she had fulfilled her child. Her one trepidation had been that he could wed. He was incredibly well known, much pursued. Yet, he had kept his heart at home. His darling, he had frequently said, was silver-haired and north of sixty. He relaxed in her support; was calmed and supported by it.

Then she had kicked the bucket, and Edith had come, and the situation had been unique.

The distinction had been exhibited in twelve ways. Edith was enjoyably warm, yet she didn't yield an inch.

"Dear Uncle Fred," she could ask, when they differ on issues of habits or ethics, or craftsmanship or games, or religion or its absence, "isn't my perspective comparable to yours?"

"Obviously my perspective is good for nothing."

"Goodness, yes it is — however you should allow me to have mine."

Her freedom met his guidelines and broke them. Her bluntness of discourse faced his well mannered reticences and the two of them talked. Frederick, obviously, accused Edith when she caused him to fail to remember his habits. They had, he held, been viewed as awesome. Edith countered that they had, maybe, never been tested. "It is adequately simple, obviously, when everyone surrenders to you."

She had brought into his home an air of innovation which horrified him. She proceeded to come however she wanted, not be limited by old principles.

"Gracious, Uncle Fred," she would agree when he dissented, "the conflict changed things. Ladies of to-day aren't sheep."

"The ladies of our family," her uncle could start, to be come by the hateful answer, "For what reason do you maintain that the ladies of your family should be unique in relation to the others you go with?"

She had him there. His refinement matched that of the others of his set. Socially he was neither a Puritan nor a Pharisee. It was exclusively under his own rooftop that he became man centric.

However, as time went on, he discovered that Edith's deficiencies were tempered by her criticalness. She didn't confide freedom and permit. She neither smoked nor drank. There was about her moving a fine and impressive quality which saved it from erotic nature. However when he told her things, there was dependably that disturbing shrug of the shoulders.

"Goodness, indeed, I'm not rambunctious, — that's what you know. Be that as it may, I like to mess about."

His pride in her developed — in her shined hair, the consuming blue of her eyes, her extraordinary excellence, the fineness of her soul, the trustworthiness of her personality. However he murmured with alleviation when she told him of her commitment to Delafield Simms. He adored her, yet nonetheless he felt the type of her presence in his foundation. It would resemble sinking once more into the advantage of a plume bed, to take up the previous lifestyle where she had entered it.

Furthermore, Edith, as well, invited her liberation. "At the point when I wed you," she told Delafield, "I will disrupt every one of the norms. In Uncle Fred's home everything runs by perfect timing, and he winds the clock."

Delafield snickered and kissed her. He resembled the other men of his age, obviously passive. However the odds were when Edith was his significant other, he, as well, would wind the clock!

Their commitment was one of shared opportunity. Edith did however she wanted, did however he wanted. They seldom conflicted. Also, as the big day drew nearer, they were charmingly careless.

Delafield, directing a letter one day to Frederick Towne's transcriber, discussed his smugness. He was writing to Bob Sterling, who was to be his best man, and who shared his loft in New York. Delafield was a vagrant, and had enormous cash interests. He felt that Washington was manageable contrasted with the city. He and Edith were to reside one block east of Fifth Avenue, in a house that he had purchased for her.

At the point when he was in Washington he was involved in a work area in Frederick's office. Lucy Logan took his correspondence. She had been for a very long time with Towne. She was 23, very much prepped, and confident. She had slim, adaptable fingers, and Delafield got a kick out of the chance to check them out. She

had delicate earthy colored hair, and her profile, as she twisted around her book, was obvious and formed.
"Edith and I are extraordinary buddies," he directed. "I rather think we will get along broadly. I'd rather not have a lady stay near my neck. Also, I need you for my best man. I realize it is asking a ton, yet it's only once in a blue moon, old chap."
That's what Lucy composed and held up with her pencil ready.
"That is pretty much all," said Delafield.
Lucy shut up her book and rose.
"Stand by a moment," Delafield chose. "I need to add a postscript."
Lucy plunked down.
"Coincidentally," Delafield directed, "I wish you'd arrange the blossoms at Tolley's. White orchids for Edith obviously. He'll know the correct thing for the bridesmaids — I'll get Edith to send him the variety conspire — — "
Lucy's pencil ran and specked. She turned upward, delayed. "Miss Towne could do without orchids."
"How would you know?" he requested.
She rippled the leaves of her scratch pad and tracked down a request from Towne to a neighborhood flower vendor. "He says here, 'Everything except orchids — she could do without them.'"
"Be that as it may, I've been sending her orchids consistently."
"Maybe she would have rather not told you — — "
"Also, you figure I ought to have something different for the wedding bouquet?"

"I figure she could like it better." There was a weak flush on her cheek.
"What might you recommend?"
"I can't rest assured what Miss Towne would like."
"What might you like?" eagerly.
She considered it genuinely — her slim fingers fastened on her book. "I think," she told him, at last, "that assuming I planned to wed a man I ought to need what he needed."
He giggled and inclined forward. "Great sky, are there any ladies like that left on the planet?"
Her flush extended, she rose and went towards the entryway. "Maybe I shouldn't have said anything."
His voice changed. "Without a doubt, I am happy you did." He had risen and presently held the entryway open for her. "We men are inept animals. I ought to never have made sense of it."
She disappeared, and he stayed there contemplating her. Her indifferent way had forever been awesome, and he had thought that she was a minimal flush enchanting.
It was a direct result of Lucy Logan, hence, that Edith had white violets rather than orchids in her wedding bouquet. Also, it was on the grounds that, as well, of Lucy Logan, that different things occurred. Three of Edith's bridesmaids were house-visitors. Their names were Rosalind, Helen and Margaret. They had, obviously, last names, yet these don't have anything to do with the story. They had been Edith's colleagues at school, and she had been fairly equitable in her determination of them.

"They are wonderful dears, Uncle Fred. I'll have three cavern inhabitants to adjust them. Socially, I assume, it will be an instance of sheep and goats, however the goats are — sweetheart."

They were, be that as it may, them six, what Delafield called a lot of delights. Their bridesmaid outfits were wonderful — however inconspicuous. The variety plot was blue and silver — and the blossoms, forget-me-nots and sweet peas. "It's a piece dated," Edith said, "however I can't stand electrifying impacts."

Neither the sheep nor the goats concurred with her. Their thoughts were unique — the goats waiting for something impressionistic, the sheep for stately quality.

There was to be a wedding breakfast at the house. Things were subsequently given over right on time to the decorators and food providers, and espresso and rolls were served in everyone's room. Late wedding presents continued to come, and Edith and her marriage chaperons may be seen consistently on the steps or in the lobby in smooth morning coats and delightful covers.

While the wedding bouquet showed up Edith searched out her uncle in his concentration on the subsequent floor.

"Take a gander at this," she expressed; "how on earth did it happen that he sent white violets? Did you tell him, Uncle Fred?"

"No."

"Sure?"

"Swear on my life."

They told their kid about Del's orchids. "Assuming he knew how I detested them," Edith would agree, and Uncle Fred could reply, "How about you tell him?"

Yet, she had never told, in light of the fact that after all it didn't matter a lot, and assuming Delafield felt that orchids were the legitimate thing, why tangle up his psyche with her inclinations?

"At any rate," she said now, "I'm happy my wedding bouquet is unique."

As she remained there, wonderful in her sheer curtains, the fragrant mass of blossoms in her arms, her eyes took a gander at him over the top, contemplatively. "Uncle Fred," she asked, startlingly, "do you cherish me?"

"Obviously — — "

"Kindly don't say it that way — — "

Her voice got.

"How might I say it?"

"As though you — minded."

He stood up and put his hands on her shoulders. "My dear kid," he said, "I do."

"You've been no closure great to me," she said, and dropped the bouquet on a seat and stuck to him, crying.

He embraced her and calmed her.

"Being a lady is a piece of hardship." She gestured. "What's more, I mustn't allow my eyes to get red."

She kissed him bashfully on the cheek. They had never revealed a lot of kisses. He felt on the off chance that she had forever been as pleasantly ladylike, he ought to have been sorry to have her wed.

He didn't see her again until she was in her wedding outfit, made and grinning.

"Has Del hit you up?" he asked her.

"No, for what reason would it be a good idea for him?"

He snickered. "Goodness, indeed, you'll have a lot to tell each other a while later." But the idea meddled that with such a lady a man could show himself, on this day of days, impassioned and energetic.

Rosalind and Helen and Margaret, sparkling, opalescent, their young eyes brilliant under their wide caps, joined different bridesmaids in the extraordinary limousine which was to take them to the congregation. Cousin Annabel went with different cousins. Edith and her uncle were separated from everyone else in their vehicle. Frederick's man, Briggs, who had been the family coachman in the times of ponies, drove them.

Washington was sparkling under the colder time of year sun as they spun through the roads to the old church.

"Cheerful is the lady the sun gleams on," said Frederick, feeling rather stupid. It was to some degree hard to talk normally to this grinning excellence in her wedding white. She appeared miles removed from the forceful lady with whom he had battled and made up and battled once more.

The wedding party was held in one of the side rooms. Late visitors streamed in a slight stream towards the extraordinary entryways that opened and closed to concede them to the fundamental hall. A gathering of workers, weighed down with wraps,

remained at the foot of the steps. When the parade began they would go up into the exhibition to see the function.
In the little room there was a practically overwhelming scent. The bridesmaids, in the separated light, were a haze of rose and blue and white. There was a lot of chuckling, the organ through the thick walls. Then, at that point, the attendants came in.
"Where's Del?"
The husband was, it appeared, postponed. They paused.
"Will we phone, Mr. Towne?" somebody asked finally.
Frederick gestured. He and his niece stood separated from the rest. Edith was grinning yet wanted to sit quiet. She appeared to be isolated from the others by the reality of the oncoming secret.
The giggling had stopped; over the murmurs came the quivering reverberation of the organ.
The attendant who had gone to the phone returned and drew Towne to the side.
"Something doesn't add up about it. I can't get Del or Bob. They might be coming. In any case, the assistant appeared to be hesitant."
"I'll go to the telephone myself," said Frederick. "Where could it be?"
In any case, he was saved from the work, for somebody, watching at the entryway, said, "Here they come," and the room appeared to murmur with alleviation as Bob Sterling entered. Nobody was with him, and he wore a stressed scowl.

"May I address you, Mr. Towne?" he inquired.
Edith was remaining by the window watching out at the old churchyard. The anxiety which had tainted the others had not contacted her. Thin and white she stood pausing. In no time flat Del would stroll up the walkway with her and they would be hitched. To her that program was essentially as fixed as the stars. Furthermore, presently her uncle drew nearer and said something. "Edith, Del isn't coming — — "
"Might it be said that he is sick?"
"I wish to Heaven he were dead."
"What do you mean, Uncle Fred?"
"I'll tell you — by and by. Be that as it may, we should move away from this — — "
His look took in the changed scene. A scourge had cleared over those high youthful heads. Two of the bridesmaids were crying. The attendants had moved into a clustered gathering. The workers were gazing — unsure what to do.
Someone got Briggs and the large vehicle to the entryway.
Close into it, Towne told Edith:
"He's pulled out of it. He left — this."
He had a note in his grasp. "Bouncing Sterling was composed. Bounce was with him at breakfast time, and when he returned, this was on Del's bureau."
She read it, her blue eyes hot:
"I can't proceed with it, Bob. I know it's a spoiled stunt, however time will demonstrate that I am correct. Also, Edith will express gratitude toward me.
"Del."

She squashed it in her grasp. "Where has he gone?"
"South, likely, on his yacht."
"Wasn't there any word for me?"
"No."
"Is there some other — lady?"
"It appears as though it. Sway is totally adrift. So is every other person."
Every last bit of her yet her eyes appeared to be frozen. The incredible bouquet lay at her feet where she had dropped it. Her hands were gripped.
Towne laid his hand on hers. "My dear — it's terrifying."
"Don't — — "
"Don't what?"
"Be grieved."
"In any case, he's a dog — — "
"It is not great to call him names, Uncle Fred."
"I figure you should view it as an extraordinary getaway, Edith."
"Escape from what?"
"Despondency."
"How about I at any point escape from the possibility of this?" The solid range of her arm appeared to demonstrate her wedding luxury.
He sat in troubled quietness, and out of nowhere she giggled. "I could have known when he continued to send me orchids. At the point when a man cherishes a lady he knows the things she enjoys."
The fact that Towne committed his error makes it then. "You should send up a little prayer of thanks — — "
She blasted out at him, "Uncle Fred, assuming you say much else like that, — it's completely imbecilic. Yet, you won't confront realities. Your age won't

ever do. I'm not at all grateful. I'm basically irate."

There was a crazy note in her voice, however he was oblivious to the pressure. She was not accepting it in that frame of mind as he wished she may. She ought to have sobbed on his shoulder. Dissolved to tears he could have alleviated her. Yet, there were no tears in those blue eyes.

She trample on her blossoms as she leaves the vehicle. Gazing directly in front of her she climbed the means. Inside everything was in preparation for the wedding celebrations. The flight of stairs was terraced with hydrangeas, pink and white and blue. In the drawing-room were rose laurels with drifting strips. Furthermore, there was a vista of the lounge area — with the caterer's men as of now at their posts.

With the exception of these men, a servant or two — and a criminal investigator to watch out for things, the house was unfilled. Everyone had gone to the wedding, and as of now everyone would return. The house would be stripped, the blossoms would blur, the cooks would divert the squandered food.

Edith halted at the foot of the steps.

"How could they report it at the congregation?"

"That it had been delayed. It was the main thing to do right now. Obviously there will be paper men. We'll need to make up a story — — "

"We'll not do anything of the sort. Come clean with them, Uncle Fred. That I'm not — needed. That I was kept — pausing — at the congregation. Like the courageous woman in a film."

She remained on the means above him, peering down. She was basically as white as her dress.

"I would rather not see anyone. I wouldn't fret losing Del. He doesn't count. He isn't worth the effort. In any case, might you at any point envision that any man — any man, Uncle Fred, might have kept me — pausing?"

## Section V

## THE UGLY DUCKLING

Frederick Towne escaped his niece's flight. "She wouldn't allow anyone to identify with her. Just locked the entryway of her room, and toward the beginning of the day she was no more. It has added immensely to the tattle."

His audience members had, in any case, weighed him yet to be determined of understanding and compassion, and had thought that he was needed. The adolescent in them agreed with Edith. However, no part of this displayed in their way. They were amenable and accommodating to the last. Frederick, guided out into the tempest by Baldy, actually saw Jane like a bird, warm in her home.

"You see," Baldy shared with his sister, when he returned, "how he wrecked things."

Jane gestured. "He doesn't have the foggiest idea — — "

"Apathetic" — Baldy's voice appeared to approach every one of the divine beings to tune in, "you ought to see her eyes — — "

"Indeed, he's fairly an old dear," said Jane, and having in this way arranged breezily of the incomparable Frederick Towne, she approached the house setting things to appropriate for the evening.

"Merrymaid out," she told her sibling; "you would be wise to get her."

He opened the entryway and the tempest appeared to spin in upon him. He called the old feline and was by and by mindful, as he remained on the patio, that she moved about him out of the loop. He pursued her aimlessly, and finally got his hands on her. She was wet to the thighs, where she had swam in the floats, yet excited like a little electric engine by the serious chill of the evening.

The breeze screeched and appeared to shake the world. Before Baldy went into the house he turned and confronted the evening — "Edith" was his voiceless cry, "Edith — Edith — — "

By morning the brutality of the tempest had spent itself. Be that as it may, it was still sharply cold. The snow was blue underneath the heavy sky. The chickens, denied their acclimated promenade, ate and drank and nodded off again in the bizarre nightfall. Merrymaid and the little cat having stuck their noses into the cold air pulled out to the cozy sanctuary of a crate underneath the kitchen oven. Sophy sent word that her stiffness was more awful, and that she was unable to come over. Jane, reviewing the collected heaps of dishes, felt a feeling of uncommon despondency. While Frederick Towne had talked the previous evening she had gotten a brief look at his reality — the extraordinary house — six workers — gay young ladies in the excitement of good garments, young fellows who matched the young ladies, cash to meet each crisis — a world wherein no one needed to wash dishes — or make soup out of Sunday's dish.

She was cheered a little, in any case, by the declaration that her sibling had chosen to remain at home from the workplace.

"I'll have an attempt at that magazine cover — — "

Her spirits rose. "Wouldn't it be absolutely great assuming that you got the award — — ?"

"Not much possibility. What I want is a decent model — — "

"Also, I will not do it?" with some contemplation.

They had discussed it previously. Baldy wouldn't see prospects in Jane.

"Since you bounced your hair, you're excessively present day — — " She was, fairly, middle aged, with her straight-trimmed dresses and her straight-trimmed locks. In any case, she was a figure so natural that she neglected to speak to his creative mind.

"Editors like them in the present day, don't they?"

In any case, his considerations had winged themselves to that other lady whom his extravagant painter painted in 1,000 postures.

"On the off chance that Edith Towne were here — I'd put her on a marble seat close to a sapphire ocean."

"I'll wager you were unable to get a supervisor on the planet to check it out. Sapphire oceans and exemplary women are 1,000,000 years antiquated — — "

"They are never old-fashioned — — "

Jane shrugged, and steered the conversation in a different direction. "Dear — on the off chance that you'll dedicate yourself to everyday things briefly. To-morrow is Thanksgiving Day, the Follettes are to eat with us, and we don't have any turkey."

"Why haven't we?"

"You were to get it when you got down to business, and presently you're not going — — "

"I'm not — not for all the turkeys on the planet. We can cook chickens. That is adequately basic, Janey."

"It might appear to be easy to you. However, who will remove their heads?"

"Sophy," said Baldy. Having killed Germans in France he declined further butchering.

"Sophy has the stiffness — — "

"Gracious, all things considered, we can eat our spirits — — " Young Baldwin's temperament was one of worship.

Jane reclined in her seat and checked him out. "Your totally wonderful arrangement might fulfill you, however it won't take care of the Follettes."

With some disturbance, accordingly, he guaranteed, if all else fizzled, to himself behead the fowls. "Be that as it may, your psyche, Jane, never takes off above food — — "

Jane, with her jaw in her grasp, thought about this. "A lady," she said, "who saves a house for a writer — should secure herself to — something. Maybe I'm similar to a hostage swell

— in the event that you cut the link, I'll shoot straight up to the skies — — "
She loved that idea of herself, and grinned over it, after Baldy had left her. She contemplated whether the link could at any point be cut. In the event that the hostage inflatable could at any point take off.
So she approached her straightforward errands, putting the bone on to bubble for soup, setting up the vegetables for it — considering what she would have for dessert — with all his disdain of homegrown subtleties, Baldy was able to be fussy about his desserts — and coming at long last to her general and cleaning in the forward portion of the house.
The phone rang and she responded to it. Evans was at the opposite finish of the wire.
"Mother needs to address you."
Mrs. Follette inquired as to whether she could change her arrangements for Thanksgiving. "Will you and your sibling eat with us, rather than approaching us? Our New York cousins find that they have the day free, suddenly. They had been asked to go to a local party in Virginia, yet their lady had needed to defer it by virtue of disease."
"Will it be extremely fantastic? I don't have anything to wear."
"Try not to be stupid, Jane. You generally seem to be a woman."
"Much thanks to you, Mrs. Follette."
Jane trusted that she didn't look as certain women look. Yet, there were, obviously, others. It was well for her right now, that Mrs. Follette couldn't see her eyes.

"Also, I thought," went on the oblivious lady, "that on the off chance that you were not excessively occupied, you could go with Evans to the woods and get a few greens. I'd like the house to look alluring. Is the snow excessively profound?"

"Not at all. When will he come?"

"You would be advised to orchestrate with him. He is right here."

Evans' voice was the main unaltered thing about him. The sound of it at a significant distance generally took the days of yore back to Jane.

"After lunch?" he inquired.

"Give a personal opportunity to dress."

"Three?"

"Indeed."

At the point when lunch get-together was finished, Jane went up-steps to get into out-of-entry garments. At the foot of the steps she had a brief look at herself in the lobby. She wore a one-piece lilac cotton gown — with a little square cover, and a microscopic face cloth. It was a decent looking little dress, yet she had it for 1,000,000 years. That was the way with all her garments. The suit she planned to put on had been colored. It had been white in its most memorable manifestation. It was currently brown. There was no telling its chromatic future.

She heard footsteps in the yard, and went to open the entryway for Evans. However, it was not Evans. Briggs, Frederick Towne's driver, remained there with a crate in his arms. "Mr. Towne's commendations," he said, "and will I set it in the lobby?"

"Gracious, indeed, thank you." Her unexpectedness carried a fast tone to her cheeks. She watched him return down the porch, and enter the vehicle, then, at that point, she opened the case.

Underneath billows of white tissue paper she happened upon a long, low container, stacked with grapes and tangerines, peaches and pomegranates. Wrapped up between the natural products were shelled nuts in fluted paper cases, glimmering desserts in little glass containers, sweetened pineapples and cherries, lots of fat raisins, stuffed dates and prunes.

Jane conversed with the unfilled air.

"How dear of him — — "

The white tissue paper fell in floats about her as she lifted the crate from the case.

There was a little note attached to the handle. Towne's own paper was thick and white. Jane knew about its cost and it excited her. His content was weighty and dark — the note had, undeniably, an air.

"Dear Miss Barnes:

"I can't let you know the amount I partook in your cordiality the previous evening — and you were great to pay attention to me with such a lot of compassion. I'm trusting that you'll allow me to come back once more and discuss Edith. May I? Furthermore, here's a touch of variety for your Thanksgiving feast.

"Thankfully generally,

"Frederick Towne."

Jane stood gazing down at the agreeable words. It didn't appear sensibly that Frederick Towne implied that he needed to come — to see her. What's more, she truly hadn't tuned in with compassion. In any case, — goodness, obviously, he could come. Furthermore, it was grand to have a thing like this occur on a day like this. As she fixed up with the container in her grasp, she saw herself again in the long mirror — a slim figure in green — bounced dark hair — brilliant and purple natural products. Once more, she heaved and looked. There was Baldy's image prepared in his hand — November! Against a foundation of dim — that gleaming figure — Baldy could romanticize her — make the breeze blow her skirts a little — give her a rippling lace or two, a celebrated exquisiteness.

She looked for him in his studio. "I have something to show you, sweetheart dear."

He was grouchy. "Try not to hinder me, Jane."

She messed up his hair, which he loathed. "Mr. Towne sent us some organic products, Baldy, and this." She held out the note to him.

He read it. "He doesn't let out the slightest peep about me."

"No, he doesn't," her eyes were moving; "Baldy, it's your younger sibling, Jane."

"You didn't do a thing yet stay there and sew — — "

"Maybe he jumped at the chance to see me — weaving — — "

Baldy disregarded this in perplexed quietness.

"Where's the organic product?"

"In the house."

He rose. "I'll go in with you — — " He felt upset, deterred. The morning had been spent in drawing unclear frameworks — a range of fair hair under a blue cap — confined feet in shoes with sparkling clasps — a sack that lingered palpably without hands. At intervals he stood up and watched out at the clear snow and the dull sky. The room was adequately warm, yet he shuddered. He languished vicariously over Edith Towne. He had trusted that she could phone. He had remained at home truly for that.

His studio was in the garage and was heated by a little round stove. Jane said the garage reminded her of the Boffins' parlor—a dead line was drawn between art and utility. Baldy's rug and old couch and paints and brushes flung a challenge as it were to the little Ford, the lawn mower, the garden hose and the gasoline cans.

"I have spent three hours doing nothing," he said, as he shut the door behind him; "not much encouragement in that."

"I have a model for you."

"Where?"

"I'll show you."

He followed her in, full of curiosity. She showed him the fruit, then picked up the basket. "Look in the mirror, not at me," she commanded.

Reflected there in the clear glass, so still that she seemed fixed in paint, Baldy really gave for the first time an artist's eye to the possibilities of his little sister. In the midst of all that crashing color——!

"Gosh," he cried, "you're good-looking!"

His air of utter astonishment was too much for Jane. She set the basket on the steps, and laughed until she cried.
"I don't see anything funny," he told her.
"Well, you wouldn't, darling."
She wiped her eyes with her little handkerchief, and sat up. "I am just shedding a tear for the ugly duckling."
"Have I made you feel like that?"
"Sometimes."
Their lighted-up eyes met, and suddenly he leaned down and touched her cheek—a swift caress. "You're a little bit of all right, Janey," which was great praise from Baldy.

## CHAPTER VI

## "STAY IN THE FIELD, OH, WARRIOR!"

Mrs. Follette had been born in Maryland with a tradition of aristocratic blood. It was this tradition which had upheld her through years of poverty after the Civil War. A close scanning of the family tree might have disclosed ancestors who had worked with their hands. But these, Mrs. Follette's family had chosen to ignore in favor of one grandfather who had held Colonial office, and who had since been magnified into a personage.
On such a slight foundation, Mrs. Follette had erected high towers of social importance. As a wife of a government clerk, her income was limited, but she lived on a farm, back of Sherwood Park, which she had inherited from her father. The farm was called Castle Manor, which dignified it in the eyes of the county. Mrs. Follette's friends were among the old families who had occupied the

land for many generations. She would have nothing to do with the people of Sherwood Park. She held that all suburbs are negligible socially. People came to them from anywhere and went from them to be swallowed up in obscurity. There was no stability. She made an exception, only, of the Baldwin Barneses. There was good Maryland blood back of them, and more than that, a Virginia Governor. To be sure they did not care for these things; old Baldwin's democracy had been almost appalling. But they were, nonetheless, worthwhile.

Mr. Follette, during his lifetime, had walked a mile each morning to take the train at Sherwood Park, and had walked back a mile each night, until at last he had tired of two peripatetic miles a day, and of eight hours at his desk, and of eternally putting on his dinner coat when there was no one to see, and like old Baldwin Barnes, he had laid him down with a will.

At his death all income stopped, and Mrs. Follette had found herself on a somewhat lonely peak of exclusiveness. She could not afford to go with her richer neighbors, and she refused to consider Sherwood seriously. Now and then, however, she accepted invitations from old friends, and in return offered such simple hospitality as she could afford without self-consciousness. She might be a snob, but she was, to those whom she permitted to cross her threshold, an incomparable hostess. She gave what she had without apology.

She had, too, a sort of admirable courage. Her ambitions had been wrapped up in her son. What her father might have been, Evans was to be. They had scrimped and saved that he might go to college and study law. Then, at that first dreadful cry from across the seas, he had gone. There had been long months of fighting. He had left her in the flower of his youth, a wonder-lad, with none to match him among his friends. He had come back crushed and broken. He, whose career lay so close to his heart—could now do no sustained work. Mentally and physically he must rest. He might be years from getting back. He would never get back to gay and gallant boyhood. That was gone forever.

Yet if Mrs. Follette's heart had failed her at times, she had never shown it. She was making the farm pay for itself. She supplied the people of Sherwood Park and surrounding estates with milk. But she never was in any sense—a milkwoman. It was, rather, as if in selling her milk she distributed favors. It was on this income that she subsisted, she and her son.

It was because of Mrs. Follette's social complexes that Jane had been forced to limit her invitations for the Thanksgiving dinner. She would have preferred more people to liven things up for Evans and Baldy, but Mrs. Follette's prejudices had to be considered.

Evans, democratic, like his father, laughed at his mother's assumptions. But he rarely in these days set himself against her. It always involved a contest, and he was tired of fighting. That was why he had asked Jane to help him in the stand he had taken against the New York trip. He felt that he could never hold out against his mother's arguments.

"She'd keep eternally at it, and I'd have to give in," he told himself with the irritability which was so new to him and so surprising. As a boy he had been good-tempered even in moments of disagreement with his mother.

Going down to luncheon, he hoped the subject would not come up. The afternoon was before him, and Jane. He wanted no cloud to mar it.

On the steps he passed Mary, his mother's maid, making the house immaculate for the guests of to-morrow. She was singing an old song, linking herself musically with the black men of generations back. Mary was over sixty, and her voice was thin and piping. Yet there was, after all, a sort of fierce power in that thin and piping voice.

"Stay in the field',
Stay in the field', oh, wah-yah—
Stay in the field'
Till the watch is over."

Again Evans felt that sense of unaccountable irritation. He wished that Mary wouldn't sing....

Later as he and Jane swung along together in the clear cold Jane said: "I've such a lot to tell you——"

She told it in her whimsical way—Baldy's adventure, Frederick Towne's visit, the basket of fruit.

"Baldy is simply mad about Edith Towne. He hasn't been able to talk about anything else. Of course, he'll have to get over it but he isn't looking ahead."

"Why should he get over it?"

Her chin went up. "He's a clerk in the departments, and she a—plutocrat——"

"Perhaps she won't look at it like that."

"Oh, but she has men at her feet. And Baldy's a boy. Evans, if I had lovely dresses 'n' everything, I'd have men at my feet."

"Why should you want them at your feet?"

"Every woman does. We want to grind 'em under our heels," she stamped in the snow to show him; "but Baldy and I are a pair of Cinderellas, minus—godmothers——"

She was in a gay mood. She was wrapped in her old orange cape, and the sun, breaking the bank of sullen clouds in the west, seemed to turn her lithe young body into flame.

"Don't you love a day like this, Evans?" She pressed forward up the hill with all her strength. Evans followed, panting. At the top they sat down for a moment on an old log—which faced the long aisles of snow between thin black trees. The vista was clear-cut and almost artificial in its restraint of color and its wide bare spaces.

Evans' little dog, Rusty, ran back and forth—following this trail and that. Finally in pursuit of a rabbit, he was led far afield. They heard him barking madly in the distance. It was the only sound in the stillness.

"Jane," Evans said, "do you remember the last time we were here?"

"Yes." The light went out of her eyes.

"As I look back it was heaven, Jane. I'd give anything on God's earth if I was where I was then."

All the blood was drained from her face. "Evans, you wouldn't," passionately, "you wouldn't give up those three years in France——"

He sat very still. Then he said tensely, "No, I wouldn't, even though it has made me lose you—Jane——"

"You mustn't say such things——"

"I must. Don't I know? You were such an unawakened little thing, my dear. But I could have—woke you. And I can't wake you now. That's my tragedy. You'll never wake up—for me——"

"Don't——"

"Well, it's true. Why not say it? I've come back a—scarecrow, the shadow of a man. And you're just where I left you—only lovelier—more of a woman—more to be worshiped—Jane——"

As he caught her hand up in his, she had a sudden flashing vision of him as he had been when he last sat with her in the grove—the swing of his strong figure, his bare head borrowing gold from the sun—the touch of assurance which had been so compelling.

"I never knew that you cared——"

"I knew it, but not as I did after your wonderful letters to me over there. I felt, if I ever came back, I'd move heaven and earth." He stopped. "But I came back—different. And I haven't any right to say these things to you.

I'm not going to say them—Jane. It might spoil our—friendship."

"Nothing can spoil our friendship, Evans——"

He laid his hand on hers. "Then you are mine—until somebody comes along and claims you?"

"There isn't anybody else," she turned her fingers up to meet him, "so don't worry, old dear," she smiled at him but her lashes were wet. Her hand was warm in his and she let it stay there, and after a while she said, "I have sometimes thought that if it would make you happy, I might——"

"Might—love me?"

"Yes."

He shook his head. "I didn't express it for that. I just needed to have reality between us. Furthermore, I don't need — feel sorry for. On the off chance that — assuming I at any point get back — I'll make you love me, Jane."

There was a touch of his old unbelievability — and she was excited by it.

She pulled out her hand and stood up. "Then, at that point, I'll — implore — that you — get back — — "

"Do you mean it, Janey?"

"I mean it, Evans."

"Then, at that point, ask great and hard, my dear, for I will make it happen."

They grinned at one another, however it was a consecrated second.

The things they did after that were delivered irrelevant by the murkiness of charm which loomed over Evans' disclosure. No man can see a lady that he cherishes her, no lady can tune in, without a pounding feeling of the greatness of what has occurred. From such starting points is composed the historical backdrop of humankind. Somewhere down in an empty where the breeze had cleared up the snow, and left the ground exposed they found crowfoot in an emerald cover — there were holly branches dribbling red berries like blood on the white floats. They filled their arms, and finally they were all set.

Evans whistled for Rusty yet the little canine didn't come. "He'll track us down; he knows every last bit of the way."

Yet, Rusty didn't track them down, and they were on the edge when that first horrendous cry came to them.

Jane grasped Evans. "What is it — gracious, what is it?"

He gulped two times before he could talk. "It's — Rusty — one of those steel traps" — he was gasping now — his brow wet — "the negroes put them around for bunnies — — " Again that furious cry broke the quietness. "They're horrible things — — "

Jane started to run toward the sound. "Come on, Evans — gracious, come fast — — "

He staggered after her. Finally he got at her dress and held her. "On the off chance that he's harmed I can't handle it."

Seeing him was appalling. Jane felt as though gripped by a bad dream. "Remain here, and relax. I'll get him out — — "

It was something horrible to confront. There was blood and that little shudder body. The cry diminished now to a struggling whining. How she opened the snare she never knew, yet she opened it, and made a gauze from her pullover which she tore from her shoulders no matter what the virus. Furthermore, after what appeared to be ages, she stumbled back to Evans with her unpleasant weight enveloped by her cape. "We must get him to a veterinarian. Get down to the street and check whether there's a vehicle in sight."

There was a vehicle, and when Evans halted it, two men came energizing the bank. Jane gave the canine into the arms of one of them. "You'll need to go with them, Evans," she said and wrapped herself all the more intently in her cape. "There are a few specialists at Rockville. You would be wise to get some information about the veterinary."

After they had gone, she remained there on the edge and watched the vehicle concealed. She felt paralyzed and crazy. It had been horrendous to see Rusty, however the most over the top dreadful thing was that vision of Evans staggering through the snow. A wrecked body is for tears — a messed up soul is past tears.

She shivered and squeezed her hands against her eyes. Then, at that point, she went down the slope and across the street in the obscuring sundown. She crawled into the house. Baldy should not see her; there was blood on her cape and her garments were torn, and Baldy would get clarification on some pressing issues, and he would consider Evans a — coward....

It was late when Evans came to Castle Manor with his canine in his arms. Corroded was agreeable and he had swayed a thankful tail. The aggravation had left his eyes and the veterinarian had expressed that in a couple of days the injury would recuperate. There were no crucial parts impacted — and he would give some medication which would forestall further affliction.

Mrs. Follette was out, and old Mary was in the kitchen, singing. She halted her melody as Evans came through. He requested that she help him and she brought a square, profound crate and made Rusty a bed.

"All of you jes' put him head by the fish, and I'll look after him."

Evans shook his head. "I need him in my room. I'll deal with him in the evening."

He conveyed the canine up-steps with him, bowed adjacent to him, drew hard full breaths as the smaller guy licked his hand.

"What sort of a man am I?" Evans expressed forcefully in the quiet. "God, what sort of a man?"

Through the still house came old Mary's flimsy and channeling tune:

"Remain in the field',
Remain in the field', gracious, wah-yah
—
Remain in the field'
Till the war is finished."

Evans got up and closed the door....

## Section VII

## A FAMISHED PILGRIM

Jane was waked for the most part by the rough crow of a nervy little chicken, who sent his test to the rising sun.

However, on Thanksgiving morning, she wound up sitting up in bed in the profound obscurity — thin and white and shuddering — mistreated by some apparition of the evening.
She came to it continuously. The unusual occasions of yesterday. Evans. Her own portion in his future. Her room was frosty. She moved up, and shut the windows, lit the light on her little table, enveloped herself by a warm robe, and sat up among her cushions, to think the thing out.
The light had a yellow shade, and sparkled like a full moon among the shadows. Jane, just past the circle of light, was a ghostly figure with her dark hair and the weak blue of her outfit.
Her own portion in Evans' future? Had she truly connected her existence with his? She had vowed to supplicate that he could get back — she had swore youth, trust and consistency to his objective. Also, she had guaranteed before she had seen that staggering figure in the snow!
In the questions of sentiment, Jane's contemplations had consistently wandered. She had longed for a brave darling, a composite legend, one who ought to join the foolish boldness of a Robin Hood with the high moralities of a Galahad. With such a sweetheart one could run through life to a funneling tune. Or on the other hand on the off chance that the Galahad prevailed in her legend, to a rousing processional!
Furthermore, here was Evans, dim and withered, shaken by quakes, squeezing himself out of the spotlight

of her future. Furthermore, she didn't need him there. Goodness, not as he had been out there in the snow! However she was upset for him with a compassion that wrung her heart. She was unable to hurt him. She wouldn't. Was there no chance to get out of it? Her hands went dependent upon her face. She had a straightforward and innocent confidence. "Gracious, God," she supplicated, "make every one of us — cheerful — — "

Her cheeks were wet as she lay back on her pads. What's more, a specific serenity followed her little supplication. Things would cooperate here and there for good.... She would allow it to rest at that.

At the point when finally the chicken crowed, Jane cast off the covers and went to the windows, stepping back the drapes. There was a weak whiteness in the eastern sky — amethyst and pearl, sea blue, the day had unfolded!

Indeed, all things considered, wasn't consistently another world? Also, on this day, everything is equal. One should ponder the grateful things!

She talked about that with Baldy at the morning meal table.

Baldy sneered. "I'm not a scoundrel. It has been a spoiled year."

"Indeed, cash isn't all that matters, and we have one another."

"Cash is a ton. Also, in light of the fact that we haven't all been killed off is not a great explanation for why we ought to thank the Lord."

"Baldy, I need to say thanks to him for the easily overlooked details. Our little house, and warmth and light, and you, returning home around evening time — —"

"My dear youngster, we don't claim the house, and I'm truly not much when I arrive."

"That isn't accurate, Baldy. Furthermore, would you confirm or deny that you are appreciative that you have me?"

There was a shake in her voice, and he was not remorseless. Nor was he in a mind-set for opinion.

"What's wrong, old dear? Maintain that I should toss flower bundles at you?"

"Indeed, I do. I'm low to myself toward the beginning of today."

He saw that she would not joke about this. "Anything occurred, Janey?" he asked in an alternate tone.

"Gracious, nothing to discuss. Be that as it may, — I wish I had a shoulder to sob on, Baldy."

"Sob on mine."

She shook her head. "No. You'd be similarly soothing as a wooden Indian."

"That's what I like," fervently.

"Your goals are great. However, your brain isn't on me. It's on Edith Towne."

"What compels you to believe that?"

"Goodness, you've one ear positioned towards the phone — — "

He flushed. "All things considered, who couldn't? I need to hear from her."

He needed to hear so much that he didn't go to chapel in case he missed her call. In any case, Jane went, sat in Barnes' seat, and was grateful, as she had said, for affection and warmth and light.

All through the message, she gazed at the stained glass window which was simply over the Follette seat. It was a commemoration to two fellows who had lost their lives in France. The window showed the youthful legends as sparkling knights — and that was the manner in which individuals pondered them. They had been, truly, rather ordinary colleagues. In any case, demise had changed them. They would remain consistently according to this world as youthful and breathtaking.

Furthermore, there underneath them sat today a man who had, as well, been youthful and breathtaking. However, who was enveloped by no sparkling protection of deception. He had returned a legend, yet had been among them sufficiently long to lose his radiance. It was clearly out of line. Jane settled that she would keep in her heart generally that vision of Evans as a sparkling knight. Whoever else neglected, she wouldn't neglect.

Evans, with his mom in the seat, gazed directly in front of him. He appeared to be worn and exhausted — a dull shadow set against the splendor of those companions on the gleaming glass.

After chapel, he sat tight in the passageway for Jane. "I'll stroll down with you. Mother will ride with Dr. Hallam."

They strolled a little way peacefully, then, at that point, he said, "Corroded is agreeable earlier today."

"Your mom let me know via phone."

He limped along next to her. "Jane, I didn't rest the previous evening —

mulling over everything. It is a thing I can't comprehend. Something shocking."
"I get it. You love Rusty. It was on the grounds that you love him so much —— "
"Yet, to allow a lady to make it happen. Jane, do you recall — a long time back? That frantic canine?"
She recalled. Evans had killed it in the street to save a kid. It had been a terrible encounter, yet not briefly had he been delayed.
"I wasn't apprehensive then, at that point, Janey."
"This was unique. You were unable to see what you adored hurt. It wasn't dreadful. It was warm."
"Goodness, don't sparkle it over. I understand what you felt. I saw it in your eyes."
"Saw what?"
"Disdain."
She turned on him. "Actually you didn't. Maybe, right from the get go. I didn't understand...." She battled for discretion, however notwithstanding it, the tears moved down her cheeks.
"Don't, Janey, don't." He was in that frame of mind of regret. "I've made you cry."
She flickered away the tears. "It wasn't scorn, Evans."
"Indeed, it ought to have been. What difference would it make? No man who calls himself a man would have allowed you to make it happen."
They had come to the way under the pines, and were separated from everyone else in that still world. Jane wrapped her hand up the criminal in

Evans' arm. "Dear kid, quit mulling over everything."
"I won't ever stop."
"I believe you should guarantee me that you'll attempt. Evans, you realize we will battle it out together...."
His eyes didn't meet hers. "Do you suppose I'd let you? Indeed, you think wrong." He started to walk quickly, so staying up with him was hard. "I'm not worth the effort."
What's more, presently very out of nowhere as she had cried, she chuckled, and the snicker had a break in it. "You personally merit all that America needs to give you." She told him of the things she had considered in chapel. "You are as a very remarkable legend as any of them."
He shook his head. "All that legendary stuff is long gone, my dear. We romanticize the dead, yet entirely not the living."
It was valid and she knew it. Be that as it may, she would have rather not let it out. "Evans," she said, and laid her cheek briefly against the unpleasant sleeve of his jacket, "don't make me despondent. Allow me to help."
"You don't have the foggiest idea what you are inquiring about. You'd become burnt out on it. Any lady would."
"Why look forward? Can't we live every day?"
She had lit a fire of trust in him. "In the event that I may — — " anxiously.
"No difference either way. Start at the present time. What are you appreciative for, Evans?"
"Not much," precariously.

"Indeed, I'll let you know three things. Books and your mom and me. Express that over — without holding back."

He attempted to go into her state of mind. "Books and my mom and Jane."

She got one more thought. "It nearly rhymes with Stevenson's 'books and food and summer downpour,' doesn't it?"

"Indeed. What a man he was — bright notwithstanding passing. Jane, I accept I could confront passing more happily than life — — "

"Try not to express things like this" — they had come to the little house on the porch, "don't express things like this. Try not to think about them."

"As a man suspects — — Do you trust it?"

"I trust some of it."

"We'll discuss it to-night. No, I can't come in. Supper is at seven." He waited a second longer. "Do you have any idea what a dear you are, Jane?"

She stood watching him as he limped away. When he turned and waved. She waved back and her eyes were obscured with tears.

In Jane's next letter to Judy she told about the supper.

"I didn't have any idea what to wear. In any case, Baldy demanded my old white. In his present mid-Victorian state of mind he would like me in 'book-muslin,' on the off chance that things were made of it. It is a wispy cloth of chiffon, and I was hard up for shoes, so I badly painted a couple of dim calfskin with silver paint, and I made a level band of silver leaves for my hair.

"The impact wasn't terrible, even Baldy let it out, and Evans cited Shelley — something about 'an orbed lady with white discharge loaded.' Evans and Baldy are having an ideal blow out of Keats and Shelley. They rise above our heads. They disdain authenticity and cynicism — they say it is an infection at the core of human progress. That all sound countries are hopeful and hopeful. It is just when nations are feeble that they become negative and sharp. You ought to hear them.

"We had a scrumptious supper. It appears to me, Judy, that my psyche harps an incredible arrangement on things to eat. Be that as it may, all things considered, for what reason shouldn't I? Housekeeping is my work.

"Mrs. Follette doesn't endeavor to do anything that she can't get along admirably, and it was all so straightforward and fulfilling. In the focal point of the table was a portion of the organic product that Mr. Towne sent in a silver epergne, and there were four Sheffield candles with white candles.

"Mrs. Follette cut the turkey. Evans can't do things like that — she wore her lasting dark ribbon and pearls, and disregarding everything, Judy, I can't resist the urge to like her, however she is such a hobo riding a horse. They haven't a penny, with the exception of what she makes from the milk, yet she looks totally the woman of the estate.

"The cousins are truly chic. One of them, Muriel Follette, knows Edith Towne personally. She filled us in regarding the wedding, and how individuals are faulting Edith for taking off and are feeling awfully upset for Mr. Towne. Obviously they didn't realize that Baldy and I had at any point looked at both of them. However, you ought to have seen Baldy's eyes, when Muriel expressed things about Edith. I was terrified that he'd say something. You know how his emotions rage out of control.

"Indeed, Muriel expressed a few catty things. That everyone is certain that Delafield Simms is infatuated with another person, and that they are saying Edith could have known it in the event that she hadn't generally viewed herself as the focal point of the universe. What's more, that's what they feel assuming her heart is broken, the good thing is grieve in the chest of her loved ones. Obviously I'm not citing her precise words, however you'll understand.

"Furthermore, Baldy figures his sovereign couldn't possibly be at fault, and was nearly exploding. Judy, he strolls in a fantasy. I don't have the foggiest idea what great it will make him to feel like that. He should continuously revere a way off like Dante. Or then again was it Abelard? I generally get those grande interests blended.

"At any rate, that's it. Edith Towne rode in Baldy's Ford, and he has hitched that little cart to a star!

"Indeed, after supper, we set the victorla going and Baldy needed to hit the dance floor with Muriel. She moves very well, and I realize he appreciated it, however he wouldn't just let it out. Also, Muriel appreciated it. There's no denying that Baldy has special insight with him.

"After they had moved some time everyone played span, with the exception of Evans and me. You know how I disdain it, and it makes Evans apprehensive. So we went to the library and talked. Evans is appallingly putting himself down. I wish that you were here and that we could talk it over. However, doing it at a significant distance is hard. There should be a workable method for aiding him. Some of the time it appears to be that I can't handle it when I recall what he used to be."

Evans had carted Jane away to the library oppressively. "I need you," was all the explanation he vouchsafed as they came into the decrepit room with its jumping flares in the chimney, its book-lined walls, its overwhelming representation over the shelf.

The picture showed Evans' granddad, and underneath it was a photo of Evans himself. The resemblance between the two men was striking — there was similar square arrangement of the shoulders, similar splendid, waved hair, similar demeanor of youth and cheerful dispositions. The granddad in the picture wore a blue uniform, the grandson was in khaki, however they were, without an inquiry, cut out of the same cloth.

"You have a place here, Jane," said Evans, "on one side of the chimney, with me on the other. That is the manner in which I generally see you when I shut my eyes."

"You see me now with your eyes completely open — — "
"Indeed. Jane, I let Mother know this midday that I wouldn't go to New York. So that is settled, without your adage anything."
"What is her opinion about it?"
"Gracious, she actually believes that I ought to go. However, I'll remain here," he moved his head anxiously. "I need to be where you are, Jane. What's more, presently, my dear, we will work things out. You realize that yesterday you made a kind of — guarantee. That you'd petition God for me to get back — and that in the event that I got back — indeed, you'd allow me an opportunity. Jane, I need your requests, yet not your commitment."
"What difference would it make?"
"I'm not fit to consider any lady. At the point when I am — well — in the event that I at any point am — you can do as you suspect best. Yet, you mustn't be bound."
She sat quiet, investigating the fire.
"You realize that I'm correct, don't you, dear?"
"Indeed, I do, Evans. I considered it, as well, the previous evening. Also, it seems like this to me. In the event that we can simply be companions — without messing with — something else — it will be simpler, could it?"
"I can't see how readily I'd annoy you, as you call it. In any case, it wouldn't be fair. You are youthful, and you reserve an option for joy. I'd be a shadow on your — future — — "
"Kindly don't — — "

He dropped on the floor covering at her feet. "Indeed, we'll leave it at that. We're companions, always," he came up and took her hands in his, "for eternity?"

"Continuously, Evans — — "

"For better, for more regrettable — for more extravagant, for less fortunate?"

"Obviously — — "

They gazed into the fire, and afterward he said delicately, "Indeed, that is enough for me, my dear, that is enough for me — — " and sooner or later he started to talk in broken sentences. "'Ok, silver sanctum, here I will take my rest.... After such countless long stretches of work and quest.... A hungry pilgrim....' That's Keats, my dear. Jane, do you have any idea about food and drink?"

"Am I?" temperamentally.

"Indeed, dear easily overlooked detail, on the off chance that I had you generally by my fire I could battle the world."

At the point when Jane and Baldy arrived at home that evening, Baldy stepped all over the house, expressing things about Muriel Follette. "A young lady like that to condemn."

"She moved well," said Jane, who had removed the silver wreath, and had started off the silver shoes, and was nestled into a major seat as agreeable as a white feline.

"What right did she have to talk?"

"Individuals are saying them."

"Did she need to rehash them?"

"Sweetheart Baldy, she didn't have the foggiest idea."

"Know what?"

"How you had an outlook on it."

He paused and remained before her. "How do you have any idea about what I feel?"
"Gracious, indeed, you appear to have made yourself Miss Towne's hero."
"I've done nothing of the sort, Jane. Yet, I have a human interest in an individual animal."
"Well," said Jane, "I have a human interest, as well."
"Is it true or not that you are ever significant, Janey?"
"It's smarter to chuckle than to cry."
There was a little catch in her voice.
Baldy wound the clock, and she watched him.
"What time is it?"
"Twelve-thirty."
She yawned. "I'm hitting the sack."
The phone rang, and Baldy was getting a move on. Jane uncurled herself from her seat and listened carefully. It was a snapshot of energizing interest. Edith Towne was at the opposite finish of the wire! Jane realized it by Baldy's performing voice. He didn't talk like that to typical people who hit him up. She was gobbled up with interest.
He came in, finally, in a real sense reveling in the sunlight of good fortune. Furthermore, similarly as Jane had felt that his voice sang, so she felt now that his feet moved.
"Janey, it was Edith Towne."
"What did she say?"
"Just saw my promotion. Paper deferred — — "
"Where could she be?"
"Past Alexandria. Yet, we're not to part with it."
"Not even to Mr. Towne?"

"No. She's approached me to bring her sack, and other things."
He hurled himself entirely into a seat inverse Jane, one leg over the arm of it. He was a thoughtless and pleasant figure. Indeed, even Jane knew about his childhood and great looks.
Edith had, as it appeared, requested that he have Towne send the ring back to Delafield — to make them marry presents sent back, to have a sack loaded with her possessions.
"I will take it to her on my vehicle — — "

"What's more, you are an ideal outsider. I believe it's totally frantic, Baldy."
"Why distraught? Furthermore, she doesn't feel that I'm an ideal outsider."
"Goodness!"
"Furthermore, it is on the grounds that I am an entirely unbiased individual."
"You're not kidding."
"What compels you to say that?"
"Goodness, you know, Baldy. You're not kidding."
Briefly his eyes bursted, then, at that point, he strutted. "On the off chance that I am, what? I'd prefer love a lady like that until the end of my life than wed anyone I've at any point seen — — "
"You don't have the foggiest idea about a thing about her with the exception of that she has exquisite eyes."
She had risen, and as she remained before him there was again that impact of two youthful cockerels on the edge of an experience. Then, at that point, they were saved by their comical inclination. "Gracious, hit the

hay," youthful Baldwin told her; "you're not kidding."
She fired up the steps however before she had arrived he shouted toward her. "Jane, what are you available for to-morrow?"
She hung over the rail and peered down at him. "Friday? Feed the chickens. Feed the felines. Assist Sophy with cleaning the silver. Drink tea at four with Mrs. Allison, and three other youthful things of eighty."
"Indeed, look here. I would rather not face Towne. He'll express things about Edith — and demand she approach him — she says he will, and that is the reason she won't hit him up. Furthermore, you have more discretion than I have. You could make everything appear — sensible. Will you make it happen, Jane?"
"Do you imply that you believe I should approach him at his office?"
"Indeed. Go in with me toward the beginning of the day."
"Baldy, would you say you are evading? Or on the other hand, do you truly suppose that I am as magnificent as your words appear to imply?"
"Gracious, assuming you will put it like that."
She grinned down at him. "How about we leave it then that I am — great. Yet, assume Mr. Towne doesn't succumb to your arrangement? Maybe he won't allow her to have the pack or a check-book or cash or — anything — — "
Jane saw an unexpected and energetic change in her sibling. "On the off chance that he doesn't allow her to have it, I will. I might be poor yet

I'll ask or get as opposed to having her taken back to confront those — felines — until she needs to come."

## Part VIII

## JANE AS DEPUTY

Frederick Towne never showed up in his office until ten o'clock. So Jane was in front of him. She sat in a sumptuous external room, pausing. To one side was an extraordinary open space — with work areas confined by glass parts. The backdrop was green, so individuals at the work areas had the impact of fish in an aquarium. There was the steady staccato tap of typewriters, and from time to time a young lady got up, swam in a manner of speaking, out of one of the glass confines and to another.

The young ladies were the vast majority of them fashionable. Much preferred dressed over Jane who had on a modest dim suit and a delicate little cap of a similar variety. One of the young ladies, blond and thin, was in the closest glass box. She wore a dark serge dress and a line of ivory dabs. She shifted focus over to Jane significantly more recognized than any of the others.

At the point when Frederick came in he saw Jane without a moment's delay, and held out his hand grinning. "You've heard from Edith?"

"Indeed. The previous evening. Past time to tell you."

"Great. We'll go into my room." He drove the way, and Jane was immediately mindful of the impact of his sincere way upon the fish who had been swimming all through the aquarium. Between the hour of Frederick's entry and the second when he shut the entryway upon them, they appeared to hang suspended. She guessed a large number of them swam once more.

In the event that the external room had looked like an aquarium, Frederick resembled a backwoods — there was a plant or two and more green paper — the sparkle of old mahogany — and in one of the shadowy corners a bronze elephant. Jane was excited by a feeling of things occurring. Obviously quiet, she was internally mixed by energy.

She sat in a major cowhide seat which almost gobbled her up, and expressed her task.

"Baldy thought I would be advised to come, he's so occupied, and in any case he thinks I have more class."

She shifted her jawline at him and grinned.

"Furthermore, you thought it required propriety."

"Indeed, don't you, Mr. Towne? We truly haven't what should be done with it, and I'm certain you suspect as much. Just now we're in it, we maintain that we should do all that can be expected."

"I see. Since Edith has picked you and your sibling as ministers, you must utilize discretion."

"She didn't pick me, she picked Baldy."

"Yet, for what reason mightn't she at any point manage me?"

"She took off from you. What's more, she isn't prepared to return."

"It would be ideal for her to return."

"She thinks not. Furthermore, she's apprehensive you'll demand."
"What does she maintain that I should do?"
"Send her the pack with the cash and the check-book, and let Baldy take out a great deal of things. She gave him a rundown; there's beginning and end from latrine water to deodorant powder."
"Assume I won't send them?"
"You can, obviously. In any case, you would, will you?"
"No, I assume not. I shan't pressure her. Be that as it may, it's somewhat odd for her to trust this to your sibling. She has seen him just a single time."
"Well," said Jane, with some soul, "you've seen Baldy just a single time, and couldn't you trust him?"
She flung the test at him, and shockingly he ended up saying, "OK, I would."
"Well," said Jane, "obviously."
He reclined in his seat and checked her out. Again he knew about revived feelings. She returned half-failed to remembering ardors. Gave him back his childhood. She utilized none of the straightforward strategies for refinement. She was daring, totally alive, and notwithstanding her modest dark suit, by and large exquisite.
So it was with a demeanor of practically heartfelt test that he said, "What might you exhort?"
"I'd leave her be, similar to little Bo-Peep. She'll return home all of a sudden, Mr. Towne."
"I wish that I could think about it — in any case, it's an extraordinary solace to know that she's protected. I will give

it out that she is visiting companions, and that I've heard from her. Furthermore, presently, about the things she needs. It appears to be totally senseless to send them."
"I don't believe it's senseless."
"What difference would it make?"
"Goodness, garments have such a great deal of effect on a lady. I can totally change my sentiments by changing my gown."
"What sort of sentiments do you have when you don't dim?"
"Cool and agreeable ones — do you know the magnificent things that are dim? Pussy-willows, and ocean gulls, and blustery days — and goodness, a great deal of things" — she overviewed him nicely, "and old Sheffield, and — indeed, I can't imagine everything." She rose. "I'll leave the rundown with you and you can phone Baldy when to come for them."
"Try not to go. I need to converse with you."
"Yet, you're occupied."
"Not except if I have any desire to be."
"However, I am. I need to go to showcase — — "
"Briggs can take you over. I'll hit up the carport."
"Briggs! Could you at any point envision Briggs passing through the roads of Washington with a pound of hotdog and a three-rib cook?"
"Do you imply that you will take your bundles back with you?"
"Indeed. There aren't any conveyances in Sherwood."
He delayed the slightest bit, then, at that point, contacted her shoulder

gently with his index finger. "Look here. Allow Briggs to take you to showcase, then, at that point, return here, and we'll approach the house, get the things for lunch at Chevy Chase, and put you down, hotdogs, sacks and all, at your own entryway in Sherwood."

"Truly?" She was all sparkling brilliance.

"Truly. You'll do it then? Plunk down a second while I call Briggs."

He called the carport and went again to Jane. "I'll direct a few significant letters, and be prepared for you when you get back."

Jane, being displayed out at last by the rich Frederick, was again mindful of the interest shown by the fish in the aquarium. She was additionally mindful that the young lady in dark serge with the white dabs had risen, and that Towne was saying, "When I return you can take my letters, Miss Logan."

Yet again he went right down to the primary floor of the large structure, and Jane and her modest dim suit were under perception, this time by individuals on the walkway, as Briggs and Towne got her into the vehicle. She rode away in an extraordinary state and class. She was not exactly certain if she was truly Jane Barnes. It appeared to be substantially more logical that she was Cinderella in a mentor made from a pumpkin, and that Briggs had been transformed from a rodent. She rested up against the advantage of the grovel hued pads, and ignored the rest of the universe of walkers. Until to-day she had been one of them, however presently she rode above them — the limousine resembled some impressive vessel breaking the tides of traffic. Jane's creative mind conveyed her fear. In any event, when she came to the market the charm continued, particularly when Briggs ended up being entirely human and supportive rather than the machine she had taught him. "On the off chance that you don't care about my going in with you, Miss," he said, "I'd like it."

So Jane went through the fine old market, with its long paths splendid with the abundance of fields, nurseries, waterways, and the straight and ocean. There were red meats and red tomatoes and red apples, oranges that were yellow, and pumpkins a more profound orange. There were shrimps that were pink, and red-snappers a more profound rose. There was the gold of margarine and the gold of honey — the green of spinach, the green of olives and the green of pickles in bowls of salt water, there was the brown of potatoes spilling over in burlap sacks, and the brown of bread prepared to dryness — the brown of the plumage of dead ducks — the white of onions and the white of roses.

Jane purchased unassumingly and Briggs conveyed her packages. He even made an idea with respect to the cut of the steak. His dad, it appeared, had been a butcher.

They drove in those days for Frederick. Briggs went up for him, and got back to say that Mr. Towne would be down in a second.

Frederick was, truly, completing a letter to Delafield Simms:

"I'm expecting that you will receive your mail at the Poinciana, however I will likewise send a duplicate to your New York office. Edith has requested that I return the ring to you. I will hold it until I realize where it could be conveyed into your hands.

"Concerning myself, I can say this — that my most memorable motivation was to kill you. Yet, maybe I am excessively cultivated to accept that your passing would improve things. You should comprehend, obviously, that you've put yourself shockingly awful of fair individuals."

Lucy's pencil faltered — a flush stained her throat and cheeks — then, at that point, she composed consistently, as Frederick's voice proceeded:

"You will wind up renounced by a few of the clubs. Whatever your intention, the world sees no real reason."

He halted. "Will you read that over once more, Miss Logan?"

So Lucy read it — still with that hot flush on her cheeks, and when she had completed Frederick said, "You can secure the ring in the protection until I give you further guidelines."

A representative came in to say that the vehicle was pausing, and as of now Frederick Towne disappeared and Lucy was abandoned in the extraordinary room, which was not to her a woodland of experience, as it had appeared to Jane, however an extraordinary jail where she pulled at her chains.

She considered Delafield Simms cruising quickly to southern waters. Of those purple oceans — the bursting stars in the wonderful evenings. Delafield had told her of them. They had frequently talked together.

She turned the ring around on her finger, concentrating on the cut figure. The lady with the butterfly wings was stunning — however she didn't have the foggiest idea about her name. She slipped the ring on the third finger of her left hand. Its precious stones bursted.

She locked it by and by in the safe — then, at that point, returned and read the letter which Towne had marked. She fixed it and stepped on the envelope. Then, at that point, she composed her very own letter. She made a little ring of her hair, and secured it to the page. Underneath it she stated, "Lucy to Del — always." She kissed the words, held the snapping sheet against her heart. Her eyes were sparkling. The incredible room was as of now not a jail. She saw past imprisonment to the vast ocean.

## Part IX

## THE SCARECROW

Mrs. Allison and the three old women with whom Jane was to drink tea, were neighbors. Mrs. Allison resided alone, and the other three resided in the homes of their few children and girls. They played a card game each Friday evening, and Jane generally came over when Mrs. Allison engaged and assisted her with the rewards. They were extremely straightforward and charming old women with their very own decent feeling nobility. They profoundly disliked the reality of Mrs. Follette's socially haughty actions. The woman of the estate addressed them when she met them in the city or in a chapel, yet she never welcomed them to her home. She was, in actuality, the chatelaine, while they were simply Smith and Brown and Robinson!

Indeed, in any event, Jane had. A portion of the other youngsters disdained these old casual get-togethers, and in the event that they came, were well-suited to show it in their way. Yet, Jane was rarely hateful. She generally had a great time, and the old women felt especially glad and adolescent when she was one of them.

However, this midday Jane was late. Tea was constantly served expeditiously at four. Also, it happened that there were popovers. Thus, obviously, they couldn't stand by.

"I called Sophy," said Mrs. Allison, "and Jane has gotten down to business. I guess something has kept her. At any rate we'll begin."

So the old woman ate the popovers and drank hot sweet chocolate, and found them not generally so scrumptious as when Jane was there to share them.

Things were, without a doubt, dull. They examined Mrs. Follette, whose flaws outfitted an unending theme. Mrs. Allison let them know that the youthful Baldwins had feasted at Castle Manor on Thanksgiving. Furthermore, there had been different visitors.

"How might she bear the cost of it," was the consistent assessment, "with that unfortunate kid on her hands?"
"He's staying nearby now, hanging tight for Jane's train," said Mrs. Allison, getting hot supplies from the kitchen. "He met the early afternoon train, as well."
The old women realize that Evans was enamored with Jane. He showed it, obviously. Yet, they trusted that Jane wouldn't check him out. He was beloved and great, and had been superb sometime in the distant past. Yet, that time had elapsed, and taking into account Mrs. Follette as Jane's mother by marriage was incomprehensible!
"He's sitting up there on the porch," Mrs. Allison further educated them. "Improve the request that he come over?"
They figured she may, however her neighborly design was rarely satisfied, for as she ventured out on the patio, a long, low limousine halted before the house, and out of it came Jane in all the magnificence of an extraordinary pack of orchids, and with a man close by, whose tastefulness compared the limousine and the beautiful blossoms. They came up the way and Jane said, "Mrs. Allison, may I introduce Mr. Towne, and will you provide him with some tea?"
"For sure, I will," Mrs. Allison appeared to ascend on wings of satisfaction, "just it is chocolate and not tea."
Furthermore, Frederick said that he loved chocolate, and as of now Mrs. Allison's little family room was all in a

charming vacillate; and over on Jane's patio, Evans Follette sat, a desolate sentinel, and contemplated on the limousine, and the tastefulness of Jane's escort.

When old Sophy called to him, "You'll catch your demise, Mr. Evans."

He shook his head and grinned at her. A man who had survived a colder time of year down and dirty barely cared about this. The actual virus was not difficult to persevere. The chilly that gripped at his heart was what scared him.

The early night came on. There were lights now in Mrs. Allison's home, and inside was warmth and chuckling. The old women, energized and energetic, let each other know in glimmering asides that Mr. Towne was the incomparable Frederick Towne. The one whose name was so frequently in the papers, and his niece, Edith, had been abandoned at the special raised area. "You know, my dear, the person who took off."

At the point when Jane said that she should return home, they squeezed around her, sniffing her blossoms, expressing charming things of her beauty — implying Towne's assimilation in her.

She chuckled and shimmered. It was an euphoric encounter. Mr. Towne had an approach to causing her to feel significant. What's more, the praise of the old women added to her delight.

As Frederick and Jane strolled across the road towards the little house on the porch, a skinny figure rose from the top step and welcomed them.

"Evans," Jane reprimanded, "you want a gatekeeper. Don't you realize that you shouldn't hang out in that frame of mind like this?"
"I'm not cold."
She introduced him to Frederick.
"Could you come in, Mr. Towne?"
However, he wouldn't. He would hit her up. Jane remained on the patio and watched him go down the stairs. He waved to her when he arrived at his vehicle.
"Gracious, Evans," she said, "I've had such a day."
They went into the house together. Jane lit the light. "Mightn't you at any point feast with us?"
"I trusted you could ask me. Mother is remaining with a wiped out companion. On the off chance that I return home, I will sup on bread and milk."
"Sophy's chops will be vastly improved." She held her blossoms dependent upon him. "Isn't the scent grand?"
"Towne gave them to you?"
She gestured. "Goodness, I've been extremely terrific and beautiful — lunch at the Chevy Chase club — a lengthy drive a short time later — — " she severed. "Evans, you look half-frozen. Stay here by the fire and get warm."
"I met the two trains."
"Evans — for what reason will you do things like this?"
"I needed to see you."
"Yet, you can see me any time — — "
"I can't. Not when you are dining with elegant courteous fellows with gold-

lined wallets." He held out his hands to the burst. "Do you like him?"
"Mr. Towne? Indeed, and I like the things he accomplishes for me. I needed to squeeze myself to be certain it was valid."
"Assuming what was valid?"
"That I was truly messing with the incomparable Frederick Towne."
"You talk as though he were presenting some help."
She had her jacket off now and her cap. She came and plunked down in the seat opposite of him. "Evans," she said, "you're envious." She was as yet striking with the energy of the evening, illuminated by it, her skin warmed into variety by the quick streaming blood underneath.
"All things considered, I am desirous," he attempted to grin at her, then, at that point, happened with a dash of sharpness, "Do you have at least some idea of my thought process as I sat watching the lights at Mrs. Allison's? Indeed, as I approached the day I passed a frigid field — and there was a scarecrow amidst it, rippling his clothes, something forlorn, something terrible. All things considered, we're two sides of the same coin, Jane, that scarecrow and I."
Her stunned look halted him. "Evans, you don't have the foggiest idea what you are talking about."
He continued wildly. "Indeed, all things considered, Jane, the thing is this. A man's looks and his cash count. I'm the very man within me that I was the point at which I disappeared. That's what you know. You could have cherished me. What is left you don't

cherish. However I am a similar man — — "

As he flung the words at her, her eyes met him consistently. "No," she said, "you are not a similar man."

"No difference either way."

"The man of yesterday didn't think — dull contemplations — — "

The light had left her as though he had blown it with a breath. "Jane," he said, precariously, "I'm grieved — — "

She liquefied on the double and started to chasten him, nearly with delicacy. "What compelled you to check the scarecrow out? For what reason didn't you walk out on him, or on the other hand assuming you needed to look, for what reason didn't you wave and express, 'Cheer up, old chap, summer's coming, and you'll be at work once more'? To me there's a carefree thing in a scarecrow in summer — he moves in the breeze and appears to excursively rebel against the crows."

He fell in with her state of mind. "In any case, his disobedience is all feign."

"How would you be aware? In the event that he fends off a crow, and adds an ear of corn to a rancher's store — hasn't he satisfied his fate?"

"Goodness, to put it that way. I guess you are implying that I can fend off a crow or two — — "

"I'm not indicating, I am telling it straight out."

They heard Baldy's move toward the corridor. Jane, rising, gave Evans' head a pat as she passed him. "You are contemplating yourself to an extreme, old dear; stop it."

Baldy, sloping in, requested a point by point record of Jane's experience. "Furthermore, I took Briggs to advertise," she told him happily, halfway through her presentation; "you ought to have seen him. He conveyed my bundles — and offered exhortation — — "

Baldy had no ears for Briggs' attractions. "Did you get the things Miss Towne needed?"

"We did indeed. We went to the house and I held up in the vehicle while Mr. Towne had the sacks stuffed. He believed that I should go in yet I wouldn't. We carried her sacks out with us."

"Who's we?"

"Mr. Towne and I, myself," she added the dynamite subtleties.

"Do you imply that you've been messing with him day in and day out?"

"Not the entire day, Baldy. Part of it."

"I don't know that I like it."

"No difference either way."

"A man like that. He could fill your head with thoughts."

"I trust my head is loaded up with thoughts, Baldy."

"You understand what I mean."

"You imply that I could figure he would go gaga for me. All things considered, I don't. However, he gets a kick out of the chance to play thus do I. I trust he'll do it some more. What's more, you and Evans are a couple of croakers. Here, I've been having a great time, and you're both attempting to remove the delight from it."

They started to dissent. She flung off their conciliatory sentiments.

"Goodness, we should have supper. Among you you've ruined my day." Yet, she was excessively carefree to hold disdain, and when the espresso came she was herself once more.
After supper, Baldy called Edith, and returned to set the victrola going to a most wild tune and hit the dance floor with Jane. It was a source for his feelings. Edith ... Edith ... Edith ... was the tune to which he moved.
Then he made Jane play his backup and sang the energetic lines of a writer much mocked by the moderns:
"She is coming, my own, my sweet,
Were it very breezy a track,
My heart would hear her and thump,
Had it pain for a century dead,
Would begin and shake under her feet,
Also, bloom in purple and red."
The influxes of exquisite sound rose increasingly elevated, appeared to break over and inundate them:
"My heart would hear her and beat....
Would begin and shake under her feet,
What's more, they bloom in purple and red."
Evans, heading back home an hour after the fact, followed the way which drove underneath the pines. The old trees showed meager and dark against the moon-splendid sky. Past the pines was the field with the scarecrow. Evans could have stayed away from it by following the street, however he was attracted to it by a kind of evil fascination, and by the memory of the things he had shared with Jane.

Under the moon the scarecrow took on like never before the similarity to a man. Softly clad in straw cap and night robe, it appeared to shudder and shake in the dreary and severe evening.

Evans rested on a wall post and reviewed his phenomenal model. The air was exceptionally still — no sound except for the weak whistle of the breeze.

Then, at that point, out of the tranquility — crisp and clean — Jane's imposing voice. "The man of yesterday didn't think about dull considerations."

He appeared to respond to her. "Is there any valid reason why I shouldn't think of them? My fantasies are dead. Furthermore, gracious, my dear, what have you to do with dead dreams?"

He had figured he would be fulfilled just to have her close to him. However, he knew now that he wouldn't be fulfilled. He had known it from the second he had seen her with Towne. Continuously henceforth there would be the trepidation that she may be taken from him. Furthermore, it was Frederick Towne who could take her. He brought everything to the table. Any young lady's head may be turned.

Towne's captivation was obvious. What's more, Jane was a choice — as a main priority and soul as well as body. It was anything but a thing for a man to miss.

He was chilled deep down when finally he disappeared from the spooky figure in the straw cap. The old scarecrow appeared to incline towards him thoughtfully as he went away.... Goodness, the thing was so human — he needed to offer it cover, a warm hearth.... He flung back at it as everything he could manage, Jane's words, "Cheer up, old chap, summer's coming."

At the point when he arrived at home, Evans went without a moment's delay to the library. Corroded in his container by the fire. He lifted himself firmly and whimpered. Evans bowed close to the bushel, and held up a saucer of milk that the old canine could drink. Then, at that point, he took a book from the rack and plunked down to peruse. His mom had not returned. She had called him at Jane's that she may be late.

In any case, he was unable to peruse. He sat with his book in his grasp, and gazed toward the picture of his granddad, and at the photo of himself. Sooner or later he rose and snapped the picture from the rack, noticing it at short proximity.

What a chivalrous youthful chap he had been, and what a couple he and Jane would have made! There was no vanity in that — he would have coordinated his childhood with hers back then. Goodness, the man in the image was a fit mate for Jane!

The one who grasped the image was a mate for — no one!

With an unexpected incensed motion, he flung it from him — the glass broke against the wall when it struck. Corroded cried in his crate, his nose past the brink of it. His lord remained as still as a sculpture in the focal point of the hearth.

At the point when Mrs. Follette returned, her child met her at the entryway. Assuming that he was pale, she didn't talk about it. "I'm half-frozen, Evans; we arrived in an open vehicle."
"Plunk somewhere around the fire, and I'll get you some hot milk."
"I wish you would. I should not gamble with a virus."
The fact that she couldn't make it irrefutably true. She was up early each day, coordinating the ones who worked for her, furthermore, watching over the cautious treatment of the milk. Evans had offered, over and again, to help her, however she jumped at the chance to do it without anyone else's help. She was extremely skillful, and she had developed her own business while her child was in the conflict. It appeared best to convey it without him. She could have done without considering Evans a milkman. A lady didn't with such ease lose standing — recognized Englishwomen had gone into a wide range of occupations. The thing was to do it with air. She had chosen wisely that she should here and there separate her item from that of the conventional dairyman, so she had called it Gold Seal milk, and each container was shut with a little gold seal bearing her family peak. Evans had chuckled at her, however her insightfulness had been legitimate. She kept her cows in fine condition and sent her cards to specialists. The cards, as well, bore the gold seal. Furthermore, soon her standing was laid out. Huge vehicles halted at her entryway, and individuals who came

hoping to find an unrefined countrywoman were guided into the old library with its representations and an overwhelming foundation of books. There Mrs. Follette, in calm dark with white sleeves and collars, her silver hair high, got them. Her clients disappeared dazzled and told others. Obviously quiet on such events, Mrs. Follette was deep down energized. She had an inclination that the circumstance was likened to Marie Antoinette at Little Trianon. She was happy she had considered selling milk — it appeared to connect her inconspicuously with eminence.

She had an illustrious air now as she sat before the fire. She generally dressed for supper. Her decrepit dark outfit showed a series of white necks. She wore a line of fly dabs and her silk shoes were decorated with stream clasps. She had pretty feet — and she studied them smugly. Then her eyes ventured out past them to something that lay in a furthest corner.

She headed toward it and got it. It was the photo of Evans which had consistently remained on the shelf. The wrecked glass tumbled from it with a tinkling sound. She had it in her grasp when Evans came in.

"How on earth did it work out?"

He set the little plate cautiously on the table. "I tossed it."

"In any case, — my dear kid, why?"

He stood checking her out. She saw his pallor. "Goodness, all things considered, briefly I was a — fool."

She was not an inventive lady. In any case, she understood what he implied. Furthermore, her jaw trembled. She was at this point not imperial. She was the mother of a hurt youngster. "I trusted things may — become simpler — — "

"They become more earnestly — — "

He plunked down on the carpet at her feet as he had endured the long periods of little childhood. Her left hand with its outdated precious stone rings hung close by. He took it in his. "Relax, Mumsie, I let you know I was a — fool. What's more, it was all over in a moment — — "

She realized it was not finished, yet she drank her milk. Then she drew his head against her knees, and educated him concerning her visit and her wiped out companion. Nothing more was said to describe the image, yet all through her presentation he stuck to her hand.

## Section X

## BALDY AS AMBASSADOR

Baldy Barnes, faring forward to find Edith Towne on Sunday morning, was a figure as old as the ages — youth in journey of sentiment.

It was freezing and the mists were weighty with wind. However, neither cold nor mists could sodden his fervency — at his process' end was a woman with eyes of consuming blue. Individuals planned to chapel as he came into the city and chimes were ringing, yet as of now he rose again in country quotes. He crossed the long extension into Virginia and followed the way toward the south.

It was early and he did not see many vehicles. However had the way been loaded with engines, he would have still been separated from everyone else in that universe of creative mind where he saw Edith Towne and that first superb snapshot of meeting.

So he entered Alexandria, going through the thin roads that talk so persuasively of history. Past the town was one more stretch of street lined up with the wide stream, and finally an old side of the road motel, of red block, with a nursery at the back, desolate now, however in summer a knot of blossom, with a region of reeds and water plants, reaching out into the stream, and a low spidery boat-landing, which showed dark at this season over the ice.

For a really long time the old hotel had been abandoned, until engine vehicles had brought back its evaporated wonders. Yet again its wide entryways were open. There was nothing bombastic about it. However, Baldy knew its standing for veritable neighborliness.

He considered how Edith had kept herself concealed in such a spot. It was astounding that nobody had found her. That some sprinkle of her presence had not been given to the papers.

He tracked her down in a curious parlor up-steps. "I think," she shared with him, as he came in, "that you are awesome natured to take this difficulty for me — — "

"It isn't any difficulty." His affirmation was no more. With her cap off she was doubly great. He felt his childhood and naiveté, yet words came to him, "And I didn't do it for you, I did it for myself."

She chuckled. "Do you generally express such pleasant things?"
"I will continuously express them to you. Furthermore, you wouldn't fret. Truly," Jane would have perceived returning trust in that chicken of the head, "I'm simply a page — twanging a lyre."
They chuckled together. He was incredible tomfoolery, she chose, unique.
"You are pondering, I extravagant, how I ended up coming here," she expressed, reclining in her seat, her shined hair against its blurred pads. "Indeed, an old cook of Mother's, Martha Burns, is the spouse of the landowner. She will do anything for me. I have had every one of my dinners up-steps. I may be 1,000 miles away for all my reality is aware of me."
"I was stressed to death when I considered you out in the tempest."
"And meanwhile I was sitting with my feet on the bumper, finding out about myself at night papers."
"Furthermore, what you read was by the drove," said Baldy, slangily. "A portion of those columnists should be shot."
"Gracious, they needed to make it happen," aloofly, "and what they have said isn't anything to what my companions are talking about. It's a decision piece. Each young lady who at any point needed Del's millions is crowing over the manner in which he treated me."
The search in his eyes bothered her. "Do you truly feel that?"

"Obviously. We're an insatiable bundle."
"I could do without hearing you express things like this."
"No difference either way."
"Since — you're not insatiable. You know it. It wasn't his millions you were later."
"What would I say I was pursuing? I wish you'd tell me. I don't have any idea."
"Indeed, I think you just followed the herd. Different young ladies got hitched. So you would wed. You knew nothing about adoration — or you could never have gotten it done."
"How would you realize I've never been infatuated?"
"Isn't it valid?"
"I guess it is. I don't have any idea, truly."
"You'll know sometime in the not so distant future. Also, you mustn't at any point consider yourself a hired soldier. You're excessively awesome for that — as well — excessively fine — — "
She understood at that time that the kid was decisive. That he was not directing pretty sentiments toward her for saying them. He was saying them all in truthfulness. "It is decent of you to put stock in me. Yet, you don't have any acquaintance with me. I'm similar to the young lady with the twist. I can be, great, yet at times I am 'horrible.'"
"You can't make me think about it." He gave her a parcel of letters. "Your uncle sent these. There's one from Simms on top."
"I figure I won't understand it. I won't pursue any of them. It has been radiant to be away from things. I feel

like a free soul, looking on yet having nothing to do with the world I have left."

They were grinning now. "I can trust that," Baldy said, "however I figure you should peruse Simms' letter. You shouldn't need to let me know you haven't any interest."

"Indeed, I have," she broke the envelope. "More than that I am frantically inquisitive. I wouldn't admit it however to anybody — yet you."

"They can cut me up in little pieces — before I end my quietness."

Again they snickered together. Then she broke the mark of the letter. Peruse it to herself, then read it a second time out loud.

"Now that it is everywhere, Edith, I need to let you know how it worked out. I realize you think it is something spoiled I did. However, it would have been more terrible assuming I had hitched you. I'm enamored with another lady, and I didn't find it out until the day of our wedding.

"She isn't in that frame of mind to blame, and some way or another I can't feel that I am a remarkable scoundrel that everyone is calling me. Things are greater at times than ourselves. Destiny just took me that morning — and cleared me away from you.

"It isn't her shortcoming. She wouldn't disappear with me, despite the fact that I beseeched her to make it happen. Furthermore, she was obviously right.

"She is poor, yet she isn't marrying me for my cash. The world will say she is — however the world doesn't perceive the genuine article. It has come to me, and in the event that it at any point comes to you, you will say thanks to me for this — however presently you'll despise me, and I'm grieved. You're a delightful, great lady — and I track down no real reason for myself, with the exception of the one that it would have been a wrongdoing in light of the current situation to attach us to one another.

"Despite everything,

"Loyally,

"Del."

There was a second's quiet, as she wrapped up. Then, at that point, Edith said, "So it's as simple as that," and tore the letter into little shreds. Her blue eyes were like pieces of steel.

"He's right," said Baldy. "I might want to kill him for making you despondent — however the thing was greater than himself."

She shrugged her shoulders.

"Obviously in the event that you will overlook — disrespect — — "

He was inclining forward embracing his knees. "I'm not overlooking anything. In any case, — I know this — that sometime assuming you at any point experience passionate feelings for, you'll excuse — — "

"I'm not prone to experience passionate feelings for," icily, "I'm excessively reasonable — — "

He concentrated on her with his radiant dark eyes. "Goodness, no, you're not. You're not at all — reasonable. You assume you are on the grounds that the men you've met have been unfortunate sticks who couldn't make you give it a second thought — — "

"I've met probably the most recognized men in America — and a couple of them have become hopelessly enamored with me — — "

"Goodness, I know. You've had a series of darlings — you're excessively immensely wonderful not to have. Yet, they've all feared you. No stone age man stuff — or any such thing. Isn't that reality?"

"I can't stand a mountain man."

"Obviously, yet you wouldn't be aloof, and you'd end via mindful — — "

"I detest ruthless sorts — strongly — — "

He sat with his jaw in his grasp, his shoulders slouched up like a faun or Pan at his lines. "All cave dwellers aren't severe sorts. Sometimes I will portray a man stealing a lady. What's more, I will make him a thin youthful god — and she will be a somewhat significant goddess — however she'll go with him — his soul will vanquish her — — "

She saw him in shock. "Then you paint?"

"I'll say I do. Awful things — magazine covers. However, in my sub-conscience there are works of art — — "

He was an eccentric youth, she chose. However, no closure is intriguing. "I don't really accept that your things are awful. Furthermore, I will need to see them — — "

"You will see them. I have a studio in our carport. I can't help thinking about what occurs around evening time when my little Ford is abandoned with my dreams. It should feel that it is battling villains — — "

He served to express, "I'm essentially as loquacious as Jane. Kindly don't allow me to discuss myself."

"Is Jane your sister?"

"Indeed. Furthermore, presently how about we get down to real factors. Your uncle maintains that you should get back home."

"I'm not going. I know Uncle Fred. He'll cause me to feel like I brought an intellectual back. He'll kill the fatted calf, yet I'll continuously realize that there were husks — — "

"What's more, pigs," Baldy enhanced, groggily. "Certain individuals are that way."

"He's forever been revered by ladies. What's more, I didn't fall at his feet. That is the reason we didn't get on. He managed his mom and his workers — and he was unable to control me. Furthermore, he'd take off to his affinities to be console, and they'd let him know a feline I — — "

"Affinities?"

"Goodness, I call them that, since there has forever been a parade of them. Ladies he reveres for the occasion. Be that as it may, it never endures, and they ruin him to death — and I won't over-indulge him. I like my own particular manner, as well, here and there, and I battle for it. Furthermore, I am the main individual on the planet who causes Uncle Frederick to blow his top. Also, he can't stand that. His habits are wonderful, generally speaking, however he essentially explodes when we get into a contention."

She was not a goddess — she was strongly human — a spirit battling to be free, and he needed to help her battle.

"Look here," he said abruptly, "assuming I were you I'd return."

"I will not."

"I figure you should. Face things out. Allow your uncle to comprehend that there are to be no postmortems. It is the main thing to do. You can't remain here until the end of time."

"Did Uncle Fred make you his diplomat?" icily.

"He didn't really. At the point when I came, I felt that I would successfully get you far from home as long as you loved. In any case, I don't feel as such at this point. You'll simply stay here and develop mad about it — rather than saying thanks to God kneeling down."

He flung it at her, suddenly. There was a second's serious quiet. Then he said, "Gracious, I really want to believe that you don't think I am teaching — — "

"No — no — — " and unexpectedly her head went down on her arm, that delightful shined head.

She was crying!

"Please accept my apologies," he told her, huskily.

Also, again there was quiet.

She chased after her hanky, and he gave her his. "You shouldn't need to be heartbroken," she said; "it appears — somewhat reviving to have somebody make statements like that. Gracious, I keep thinking about whether you know how hard we are — and critical — individuals of my set.

What's more, I don't accept any of us ever — say thanks to God."
She cleaned her eyes, tracked down her own tissue, and gave his back to him. She didn't have any idea how he cherished it — thereafter — a goblet for her tears. She found it numerous years after the fact — shut away in a case with a branch of heliotrope.
They talked for an hour after that.
"There is not a really obvious explanation for why you ought to hustle back," Baldy said, "yet I'd allow your uncle to let individuals know where you are. Then the papers will drop it, don't you see?"
"I see. Obviously I've been senseless — yet you can't think how I endured."
She could not have possibly let it be known to any other individual. Be that as it may, she met his truthfulness with her own.
"I planned to have our lunch presented here," she said, "yet I figure I will not. The lounge area down-steps is enchanting — and assuming anybody comes in that I know — I shan't really mind — for however long I'm returning."
The mammoth chimney in the old lounge area had been reestablished to old purposes. Martha and her better half had perceived its worth as a foundation, so meat was broiled on the spit — a turkey to-day as it worked out. The tables were lit by high white candles — and there were old hunting prints on the walls.
The food was scrumptious, and having settled her concerns, Edith showed herself wonderfully gay and silly.
There was a heliotrope in a Sheffield

bowl on their table. "Martha grows old-molded blossoms in pots," Edith said. She chose a splash for himself and he put it in his jacket. "It's my #1." She informed him regarding Delafield's orchids. "Consider such an extremely long time," she said, "and he never knew the blossoms I like."

There were others in the room, however it was only after the finish of the dinner that anybody came whom Edith perceived.

"Eloise Harper — and she sees me," was her unexpected comment. "Presently watch me cart it away." She stood up and waved to a party of four individuals, two men and two ladies, who remained in the entryway. They saw her without a moment's delay, and the impact of their approaching was a rush.

"Favored kid," said the young lady who was ahead of the pack, "have you absconded? Furthermore, is this the man?"

"This is Mr. Barnes," said Edith, "who comes from my uncle. I'm going to return. Yet, I have had a plugging experience."

Just Baldy realized what was in her heart, and that confronting them was so difficult. However, on a superficial level she was pretty much as shining as most of them. "I will likely be in the papers in the future to-morrow morning. You realize you will not have the option to keep it, Eloise."

Eloise, red-haired and striking in a shroud and turban of wood-brown, appeared to stand intellectually stealthily. "I wouldn't miss the

discussion I will have with the journalists to-night."
One of the men of the party dissented. "Try not to be a numbskull, Eloise."
"All things considered, I owe Edith something. Don't I, sweetheart?"
"You do." There was a fire toward the rear of Edith's eyes. "She loved Delafield before I did."
"Feline," said Eloise gently. "I preferred his yacht, yet Benny's is greater, isn't it, Benny?" She went to the more youthful man of the party who had not spoken.
"I'll say it is," Benny concurred, happily, "and it isn't simply my yacht that she's later. She has a genuine little case on me."
The subsequent lady, more seasoned than Eloise, tall and blond in smoke-dim with a breadth of dull blue wing across her cap, said, "Edith, you terrible kid, your uncle has been horrendously stressed."
"Obviously, you'd be aware, Adelaide. What's more, it makes him great to be concerned. I'm a cure until the end of you."
Everyone chuckled aside from Baldy. He ran his fingers with an apprehensive signal through his hair. He resembled a youthful falcon with an unsettled peak.
Martha came up to set up for a table.
"Carry your espresso over and sit with us," Eloise said; "we need to hear about it."
Edith shook her head. "I don't have a place with your reality yet. Furthermore, I've made some brilliant memories without you."

They continued giggling. Quiet chose the two they abandoned. Furthermore, out of that quiet Edith inquired, "You could have done without the things we said?"
"Contemptuous!"
"Do you generally show what you feel like that?"
"Jane says I do."
"All things considered, assuming it had been anyone however Eloise Harper and Adelaide Laramore. Adelaide is Uncle Fred's most recent."
She rose. "How about we go up-steps. To toss things at their heads. Also, I don't want to break Martha's dishes."
They halted at the other table, nonetheless, for a light word or two, then went up to Edith's living room on the subsequent floor. When they were again by the fire, she said, "And presently what is your take of me? Decent attitude?"
"I think," he said, speedily, "that they presumably merited it."
She laid her hand briefly on his arm. "You are somewhat dear to say that. I was truly shocked."
At the point when he was finally prepared to go, she chose, "Advise Uncle Frederick to send Briggs out for me in the first part of the day. I should have it over, now that Eloise will get out the word."
"I wish you'd go in with me — to-night."
"Gracious, yet I couldn't — — "
"Same difference either way."
She weighed it — "And shock Uncle Fred?"
"I think we would be wise to phone, so he can kill the fatted calf."

"Indeed. He could do without things sprung on him. At any point it harms his respect — yet he's somewhat an old dear, and I love him — do you fight with your loved ones?"
"Jane and I battle. Incredible times."
"I have an inclination that I will like Jane."
"You will. She's the best of all time. Not a stunner, but rather developing better-looking consistently. Weaved her hair — and I almost took her head off. In any case, she's somewhat of a peach."
"I'll have you both down for supper sometime in the future. I think we will be companions" — again that light touch on his arm.
He got her hand in his. "I will just ask that you let the page twang his lyre." Then with a more profound note, "Miss Towne, I can't let you know how much your companionship would mean."
"Could it? Gracious, I will have a few great times with you and your younger sibling, Jane. I am so burnt out on individuals like Eloise and Adelaide, and Benny and — Del...."
On this equivalent evening little Lucy Logan was keeping in touch with Delafield Simms.
"It appears as though a fantasy, darling, that you are to come for me in February, and that then, at that point, we'll be hitched. What's more, for the remainder of my life I am to have a place with you.
"Del, it isn't on the grounds that you are rich. Obviously I will revere the things you can accomplish for me. I won't imagine that I shan't. In any case, on the off chance that you were

poor, I'd work for you — live for you. Gracious, Del, I truly do trust that you will trust it.

"A day or two ago, Mr. Towne said in one of his letters that you had forever been flighty, that there had been loads of young ladies, Eloise Harper before Edith. Furthermore, I needed to shout right out and say, 'It isn't accurate. He hasn't at any point truly minded before this.' But obviously I proved unable. Yet, I broke a pencil point, and with respect to Mr. Towne, why should he express such things about you? I haven't taken his letters throughout the previous three years in vain. There's consistently someone — the last one was Mrs. Laramore, and presently he has his eye on a little Jane Barnes, whose sibling found Miss Towne's sack and the ring. She's fairly dear, however I want to believe that she won't think he is vigorously.

"What's more, presently, my dear and my sweetheart, goodbye. I can't help thinking about how I dare call you that. However, I am continuously expressing it to myself, and around evening time I request that God protect you —."

After five days, Delafield read Lucy's letter. He was on his yacht in southern waters. His man had been sent in for the mail.

At the point when he had gotten done, Delafield lay back in his patio seat and mulled over everything. An eccentric thing for him to fall like that for little Lucy. He had not accepted that it was in him to mind in that way for a lady. However, he did. The letter lay like a live warm thing under his hand. It appeared to thump with his heart as Lucy's heart had thump against his own on that last morning in Frederick Towne's office, while his lady of the hour paused.

## Section XI

## THE DIM LANTERN

Jane, in Baldy's nonappearance, ate on Sunday with the Follettes, around mid-afternoon. In the early evening she and Evans took a walk, and got back home to tea in the library. Extended in a long calfskin seat, Evans read to Jane and his mom "The Eve of St. Agnes."

"How unpleasant cold it was!
The owl, for every one of his plumes, was a-cold:
The rabbit limped shudder through the frozen grass,
Also, quiet were the group in the wooly crease."

Jane, nestled into the lounge chair in her number one demeanor, stood by listening to that unique depiction of the distinct winter climate, and was happy with the glow and comfort. She was happy, as well, of this charming organization — Mrs. Follette was an incredible dear, with her duchess air, and her commitment to Evans. What's more, Evans, perusing in that exhilarating and unaltered voice, was at his best.

With respect to Mrs. Follette, she was dependably delighted to have Jane visit them. The kid was so merry, and Evans required cheer. Then, as well, Jane was a magnificent split between the young lady of yesterday and the super present day lady who stunned Mrs. Follette by her absence of

respect as well as by her absence of hesitance.
Jane could have weaved hair, yet she didn't have a bounced hair mind. The importance of this end was very obvious to Mrs. Follette, despite how dark it very well may be to other people. Young ladies who trim off their hair, generally speaking, went farther — Jane halted at her hair.
Then, as well, Jane had what may be called dated homegrown characteristics. She kept her little house as spotless as she kept herself. In winter everything was shiny and splendid; in summer fresh drapes waved in the warm breeze; there were cool shadows inside the perfect, calm rooms.
Right now, Mrs. Follette was weighing truly the reality of Jane as a spouse for Evans. She was pretty as well as bright. I had great habits. Obviously, in the past, Evans would, unavoidably, have looked higher. There had been a lot of rich young ladies anxious to draw in him. He had limitless solicitations. Ladies had, truth be told, very pursued him. Florence Preston had rather embarrassed herself. What's more, Florence's dad had millions.
Be that as it may, presently — — ? Mrs. Follette knew how little Evans brought right now to the table. She preferred not to just let it out, however the reality of the situation was clear. Watching the two youngsters, she concluded that should Evans care for Jane, she would erect no hindrances. Concerning Jane, marriage with Evans would be, as it were, an ascent

on the planet. She would inhabit Castle Manor rather than at Sherwood Park.

The sonnet had arrived where Mrs. Follette felt that she should dissent. She was not exactly certain that she supported the circumstance it framed. The stanza existing apart from everything else, for instance — Porphyria's supplication to the servant, old Angela:

"To lead him in close mystery,
Indeed, even to Madeleine's chamber and there stow away
Him in a wardrobe of such protection,
That he could see her excellence unspy'd
Furthermore, win, maybe, that evening, an unbeatable lady of the hour."

Deprived of all its fine words, it was what was happening.

Evidently, nonetheless, the youngsters were without self-consciousness....

"Out went the shape, as she rushed in:
Its little smoke in gray home brew kicked the bucket — — "

Evans turned upward. "Might there be anything lovelier than that last line?"

Jane's eyes had dreams in them. "Try not to stop," she said.

He read on.... "She shut the entryway ..." his voice took a more profound note.

"Rose-sprout fell on her hands, together prest,
Furthermore, on her silver cross delicate amethyst,
Furthermore, on her hair a magnificence like a holy person:

She appeared to be a marvelous holy messenger, recently drest,
Save wings for paradise; Porphyro developed faint:
She bowed so unadulterated a thing, so liberated from mortal impurity."
"Evans," said his mom, as he stopped once more, "that sonnet doesn't appear to me precisely legitimate."
He gave her a shocked look. "Try not to indulge it for us, Mumsie."
"Gracious, well," Mrs. Follette shrugged her pleasant shoulders, "we won't contend. In any case, when I was a young lady we didn't pursue things like that."
"However, this was composed before you were a young lady."
"Why does that matter?"
"Yet, the wealth and variety. You see it, Jane, don't you?"
"Indeed. Finish it, Evans."
What's more, when he reached the end, she said, "If by some stroke of good luck life were that way."
"Like what?"
"High sentiment. Porphyro says carelessly, 'For o'er the southern fields I have a permanent spot for you.' But admirers of to-day need to consider lease and food and garments. Also, lodging bills for the wedding trip."
"Gracious, you ladies" — he sat up blazing — "would you say you are scheming to over-indulge my sonnet? Jane, it is the fantasies of people which shape their lives."
As his eyes met hers something mixed inside her like the ripple of a bird's wings lifted to the sun....
It was after five when Baldy called victoriously: "Jane, Edith Towne has

consented to return home to-night. Also, I'm going to take her. I called up Mr. Towne and told him and he maintains that you should be there when we come. He'll send Briggs for yourself and we are all to eat together."
"Yet, Baldy, I don't know Edith Towne. For what reason doesn't he request some from her own companions?"
"She doesn't need them. Loathes them all, and at any rate he has asked you. Why stress?"
"I'll need to return home and dress."
"All things considered, you're to tell him immediately where Briggs can get you. I let him know you were at the Follettes'."
Jane returned and rehashed the discussion to Evans and his mom. Mrs. Follette was greatly intrigued. The Townes were the most notable individuals. "How pleasant for you, Jane."
However, Evans contradicted her. "What compels you to say that, Mother? It isn't pleasant. It will basically be disturbing."
"I don't have the foggiest idea about why you say that, Evans," Jane contended. "I'm not effortlessly vexed."
"However, with all that cash. You can't stay aware of them."
"Try not to place thoughts into Jane's head," his mom criticized; "a woman is consistently a woman."
However, Jane sided now with Evans. "I understand, Mrs. Follette. I don't have any clothes. I don't have anything to wear to-night."

"Gracious, I wasn't thinking about your looks." Evans got up and remained on the hearth-carpet. "However, that's what individuals like! Jane, I wish you wouldn't go."
She gazed toward him with her jaw shifted. "I don't have the foggiest idea how I can reject it."
"Obviously she can't. Evans, don't be so preposterous," Mrs. Follette intervened; "it will be something superb for Jane to know Edith."
"Will it be a particularly superb thing for her to know Frederick Towne?" He flung it at them.
Jane requested, "Don't you believe that I should have a great time?"
He gazed at her briefly, and when he talked it was in an alternate tone. "Indeed, obviously. I ask for your exoneration, Janey."
Mrs. Follette, having destroyed herself for the second from the discussion, concluded that things between her child and little Jane Barnes could arrive at a peak all of a sudden. "I trust he's half enamored with her," she let herself know in some bewilderment. With respect to Frederick Towne, she didn't think about him briefly. Jane was a lovely kid. However, Frederick Towne could have his pick of ladies. There would not be anything serious in that frame of mind with Jane.
Jane called up Towne. "It was great of you to ask me," she said. "I'm at the Follettes', yet I'll return home and dress and Briggs can come for me there."
"Come as you are."
"You wouldn't agree to that if you would see me. I went for a stroll with

Evans this evening and I will show its impacts."
"Evans? Gracious, Casabianca?"
"What makes you decide that?"
"I considered it when I saw him sitting tight for you at the highest point of the patio. 'The kid remained on the consuming deck — —'" he snickered.
"I don't feel that is entertaining by any means," said Jane, honestly.
"Isn't that right? All things considered, I ask for your exoneration. I'll beseech it again when I get you here. Briggs will arrive at Sherwood at around seven. I would drive out myself, however I've a dreadful cold, and the specialist lets me know I should remain in. What's more, Cousin Annabel is wiped out in bed with a cold, so you should show compassion for me and keep me company...."
Jane hung up the recipient. It would, she chose, be an astonishing experience. Yet, she didn't know that she enjoyed Frederick Towne....
Evans headed back home with her. The air was hotter than it had been for a really long time, and weak dogs had risen. The fog thickened at last to a mist which turned over them as though blown from the high oceans. However the ocean was miles away, and the haze was brought into the world in the waterways and streams, and in the softening snow.
They found it fairly challenging to keep to the street. They were nearly covered in the thick dim masses. Their voices had a muted sound. Evans' hand was on Jane's arm so they could hold together.

"Jane," he said, "I embarrassed myself about Towne. However, truly — I was apprehensive — — "
"Of what?"
"That he could become hopelessly enamored with you — — "
"He's not considering me, Evans, what's more he's excessively old — — "
"Do you truly feel as such about it, Jane?"
"Obviously — senseless."
He was unable to see her face — however the words in her giggling beautiful voice provided him with a feeling of consolation.
"Janey," he said, "in the event that I could have you like this generally. Close away from the world."
"Be that as it may, I would rather not be closed away. It would be ideal for I to feel — confined — — "
"Not on the off chance that you gave it a second thought."
There was in his tone the imposingness of serious inclination. She was moved by it. "Goodness, I understand what you mean. Yet, love won't come to me like that — shut in. I will need opportunity, and daylight. I'll be a gull over the ocean — a boat in full sail — a vagabond out and about — yet I won't ever be a phantom dazed."
His hand dropped from her arm. "Maybe you'll be a princess in a palace. Towne can make you do that."
"For what reason do you continue to bother Mr. Towne? I could do without it."
"Since — gracious, I think everyone needs you — — "

Furthermore, presently it was she who got at his arm in the fog, and rested on it. "I'm not the most un-in affection with Frederick Towne. What's more, I won't ever wed a man I don't cherish, Evans."

At the point when they came to the little house they found old Sophy gesturing in the kitchen. She generally remained with Jane when Baldy was away. So Evans said "Goodbye" and began back.

He tracked down the way between the pines, strolled a couple of steps and staggered. He plunked down on the log that had stumbled him. He had no wish to go on. His downturn was extraordinary. Night was before him and obscurity. Forlornness. Also, Jane would accompany Frederick Towne. He had for Jane a sensation of irredeemable veneration. She could never be his. For how is it that he could attempt to keep her? "I'll be a gull over the ocean — a boat in full sail — a wanderer out and about — never a phantom confused."

What's more, he was only a phantom dazed! Gracious, what was the utilization of ever "moving up the climbing wave"? One high priority is something of desire to live on. A fantasy or two — ahead.

How long he stayed there he didn't have the foggiest idea. And at the same time he knew about a pale haze against the common melancholy. And afterward he heard Jane's voice calling, "Evans? Evans?"

He replied and she came dependent upon him. "Your mom called — that

you had not returned home — and she was concerned."
She was holding the light up to the length of her arm. In her orange shroud she radiated through the cover of fog, iridescent.
"My dear," she said, delicately, "for what reason would you say you are staying here?"
"Since there isn't any utilization going on."
She brought down the light with the goal that it gleamed all over. What she saw there scared her. "Are you feeling as such as a result of me?" she asked in a shaking voice.
"As a result of everything."
"Evans, I will not go to the Townes assuming that you believe I should remain."
He gazed toward her as she twisted above him with the light. She appeared to sparkle inside and without, similar to some heavenly guest.
"Could you remain, Jane, in the event that I needed it?"
"Indeed."
He stood up. "I don't need it. Not actually. I'm not exactly a particularly self centered pig," his grin was frightful.
She was quiet briefly, then she said, "I'm returning home with you, Evans. Hold on until I advise Sophy to send Briggs after me."
He attempted to dissent, however she was firm. "I'll be back in a moment."
She returned by and by, the light in one hand and her shoe pack in the other. "I put on heavier shoes. I ought to demolish my shoes."

As they trample the way together, the illumination of the light sparkled in round spots of gold, presently before them, presently behind them. The haze squeezed close, however the way was clear.
"Evans," said Jane, "I believe that you should guarantee me something."
"Anything, with the exception of — not to adore you."
"It doesn't have anything to do with adoration for me, yet it has something to do with affection for God."
He knew how hard it was for her to say that. Jane didn't talk effectively of things like this.
She happened with some faltering. Her voice, suppressed by the haze, had a muffled note of music.
"Evans, you mustn't let what I truly do make you or break you. Regardless of whether I love you, you should go on. You — you were unable to hold me on the off chance that you weren't sufficient, regardless of whether I was your significant other. Furthermore, there is strength in you, on the off chance that you'll just trust it. Goodness, you should trust it, Evans. Furthermore, you mustn't cause me to feel capable. I can't handle it. To feel constantly that I am hurting — you."
She was wailing. Somewhat indistinguishable.
"Furthermore, you are skipper of your spirit, Evans. You. Not any other individual. I can't be. I can be an assistance, and goodness, I will assist all I with canning. That's what you know. Be that as it may, — I love you like an elder sibling — not differently. On the off chance that anything ought

to happen to you, it would be frightful for me, similarly as it would be horrendous assuming anything happened to Baldy."

"Janey, my dear, don't," for she was gripping to his arm, crying as though her heart would break.

"However, I truly do really focus on you so much, Evans. I was frenzied when your mom called. I wasn't exactly dressed and I caused Sophy to get the lamp, and afterward I ran down the way, and searched for you."

He halted and laid his hand on her shoulder. Her shortcoming, her wrecked words had stirred in him an unexpected defensive delicacy.

"My daughter," he said, "don't. God helping me, I will get back. Also, you will light my direction. Jane, do you have at least some idea when I saw you coming towards me with that faint light it appeared to be representative. Trust held out to me — seen through a haze, faintly. Yet, a light, all things considered."

"Goodness, Evans, in the event that I could cherish you, I would, that's what you know."

"I know. You'd tie up the wrecked wings of each and every bird. You'd give support to the faltering, and food to the hungry. Also, that is the manner in which you feel about me."

He had let her go now, and they stood separated, covered in spooky white.

"God helping me," he said once more, "I'll get back. That is a commitment, Janey, and here's my hand upon it."

She gave him her hand. "God helping us both," she said.

He lifted her hand and kissed it. Then, peacefully, they strolled on, until they came to the house....
The Towne vehicle was pausing, and Mrs. Follette in a whirlwind invited them. "I don't understand the reason why you didn't ride over with him."
"He hadn't come, and we liked to walk."
"What was wrong with you, Evans?"
"Not a lot, Mother. Please accept my apologies if you object." He did not give her a great reason.
Jane put on her shoes and went off in the extraordinary vehicle. And afterward Evans said, "I'm heading toward Hallam's."
"Might it be said that you are well, my dear?"
"I need to converse with him." He saw her restless look, and twisted and kissed her. "Sit back and relax, Mumsie, I'm okay."
Dr. Hallam's old domain appended the Follette ranch. The specialist was a nerve trained professional, and went each day to Washington, returning around evening time to the calm of his beguiling home. He was unmarried and was taken care of by men-workers. He had been abundantly keen on Evans' case, and had as a matter of fact had charge of it.
The specialist was by the library fire, smoking a stogie and perusing an earthy colored book. He invited Evans generously. "I was pondering when you would turn up once more." He showed the title of his book, "Boswell. There was a man. As incredible as the man he expounded on, and we are simply starting to think that it is out."

"Intriguing release?" Evans plunked down.
"Indeed. Got it at Lowdermilk yesterday."
"We've tons of old books on our racks. I should sell them, I assume."
"I wouldn't sell one of mine." Hallam was earnest. "I'd prefer murder a child."
Evans flared unexpectedly. "I'd sell mine, on the off chance that I could get the things I need."
"I need nothing, however much I need my books."
"Indeed I do. I need life as I used to live it."
The specialist sat up and checked him out. "You mean before the conflict?"
"Indeed."
"Great."
"I'm worn out from being a part of a man. Assuming there's some exit from it, I believe that you should tell me."
The specialist's eyes were brilliant with interest. He knew the first side effects of recuperation in quite a while. The neurasthenic nature of Evans' difficulty had denied him of drive. His awakening was a promising sign.
"What should be done, obviously, is to get to work. How about you open an office?"
"A fat opportunity I'd have of getting clients."
"I think they'd come."
The specialist smoked for a period peacefully, then, at that point, he expressed, "Settle on something hard to do it interminably. Do it assuming that you believe you will bite the dust in the endeavor."

There was a rousing thing to Evans in the thought. Hard things. That was all there was to it. He spilled out the narrative of the beyond couple of days. The horrendous scene with Rusty. To-night in the haze under the pines. "Believed more than anything should drop myself in the stream."

He was strolling the floor, this way and that, limping to one edge of the mat, then, at that point, limping to the next. "Then, at that point, Jane came. Little Jane Barnes. You know her, and she told me — where to get off — said I was — skipper of my spirit — — " He halted before the specialist, and grinned capriciously. "Are any of us skippers of our spirits, specialists?"

"I'll be darned on the off chance that I know." The specialist was strongly serious. "Self discipline has a great deal to do with things. The difficulty is the point at which your will won't work — — "

"Mine is by all accounts chipping away at one chamber." Again Evans was pacing the mat. "However, that thought of an office request to me. However, it will take a touch of cash. What's more, it is somewhat an issue to know where to get it."

"Sell a portion of the old books. I'll get them."

Light jumped at Evans. "It could be one way, couldn't it? Mother would prefer to not stand it. Yet, what's a library against a daily existence?" He appeared to indulge the inquiry to a listening universe.

The specialist giggled. "She'll be reasonable assuming you put it up to her. What's more, you should frivol a little. Mess with the young ladies."

"I need no young ladies with the exception of Jane."

"Little Jane Barnes. Indeed, she'll do it."

"I'll say she will."

The specialist, watching him as he strolled to and fro, said, "what to do is to delineate a typical day. Make it very near the program you followed before the conflict. You haven't ended up keeping a journal, have you?"

"Indeed. It's a cumbersome record. Mother began with me when I was a youngster."

"We need "That. Peruse it consistently, and do a portion of the things the following day that you did then. You will find you can stick nearer than you naturally suspect. Furthermore, it will give you a functioning arrangement."

Evans plunked down and examined the thought. It was late when he rose to leave.

"It will be slow," was Hallam's last caution, "yet I accept you can make it happen. What's more, when things turn out badly, simply sound and I'll loan you a few gas," his enormous snicker blast out, as they remained in the entryway together. "Frightful evening."

"I have a light." Evans got it from the patio.

At the point when Evans arrived at home his mom called from up-steps, "I thought you were rarely coming."

"Hallam and I had a ton to discuss."

He came running up, and going into her room tracked down her set up on her pads.

Mrs. Follette in bed didn't lose anything of her respect. Her silver hair around evening time was plaited and twisted into a coronet over her quiet brow. She wore something sewed in white and dark about her shoulders. There was a request book on her bedside table — and pineapple presents on her bed. She had acquired her religion and her furniture from her precursors, and she kept them both all together.

"Mother," said Evans, and stood peering down at her, "Hallam believes that I should sell a portion of the old books and utilize the cash to open an office."

"What sort of office?"

"Regulation. Around."

"In any case, would you say you are all around ok, Evans?"

"He says that I am. He says that I should believe that I am well, Mother."

"Be that as it may, — — "

"Dearest, don't over-indulge it with questions. It's my life, Mother."

There was a look all over which she had not seen since his return. Inspired, anxious. A light in his eyes, similar to the light which had sparkled according to a kid.

She found it challenging to talk. "My dear, the books are yours. Do as you naturally suspect best."

He hung over and kissed her, lifting her a piece. There was energy as well as fondness in the speedy touch. She drew herself away giggling, short of breath. "How solid you are."

"Am I? All things considered, I assume I am. Furthermore, I will vanquish the world, Mumsie."

His commendation endured during the perusing of the journal. It was a fat little book, and the pages were composed close in his fine firm content. He tracked down things between the leaves — a four-leaved clover Jane had sent him when he made the football crew. A rose, dismal and dry. Florence Preston had given it to him.

He dropped the rose in the waste-bin. How is it that he could at any point have considered Florence? Love wasn't a thing of blue eyes and pale gold hair. It was a thing of fire and fire and battling.

Battling! That was all there was to it. With your options somewhat limited — and winning!

For some time or another he intended to win Jane. Did she figure she could be on the planet and not be his? Also, assuming that she adored strength she ought to have it. He twisted his head in his grasp — his hands caught rigidly. There was a request in his heart. His entire being hurt with the desolation of his work.

"Gracious, God, let me battle and win. Take me back to the full proportion of a man."

Again he opened the book. Pieces of printed refrain exited it. Jane had sent him this, "One who never turned his back, however walked bosom forward."

All things considered, he had turned his back. That day in the snow. The idea held him. Made him white and wiped out. He stood up, supplicating again in a desolation of brain, "Bring me back."

He opened the book and read of Jane, and of himself as he had once been. He skirted the record of his school days, with the exception of where he tracked down such a reference as this: "Little Jane is growing up. She met me at the station and held out her hand to me. I consistently used to kiss her, yet this time I didn't even think about it. She was different in some way, yet some time or another I'll kiss her." Furthermore, this: "Jane is somewhat a sweetheart. Yet, I am starting to accept that I like them fair." That was the point at which he had eyes for Florence Preston, whose shading was blue and gold. Be that as it may, it hadn't endured, and he had returned to Jane with a feeling of reward.

He found that the pages had finally surrendered to those first days after he had been owned up to the Washington bar, and had hung out his shingle.

"Sat at my work area all morning. Extraordinary feign. One client got an extraordinary impact of occupiedness. Eaten with a great deal of colleagues — hotcakes and wieners — ate an armful. Tea with three débutantes at the Shoreham — peaches. Dance at the Oakleys' in Georgetown. Plugging time. One dangerous second when the head servant took my jacket. Needy individuals should not move where there are head servants."

Recollecting that episode, he reclined in his seat and snickered. The Oakleys had all the cash on the

planet, and a foundation of privilege. Evans' jacket was corroded and gleaming at the elbows. The steward, a new import from London, had been forcing in knee-breeches and many buttons. His way had been great, yet Evans had known about the worker's disdain of corrosion and gloss. Then, at that point, his own excellence had acted the hero, and he had gone in and had hit the dance floor with as light heels as most of them.
He tracked down more than one reference to his destitution. "I will need to quit eating, or I can't wear my night clothes. Also, I can't manage the cost of new ones. Jane says she would rather not have me get thinner — that I look large and lovely presently like Michelangelo's David at the Corcoran. I don't know whether she is energetic or not. One won't ever be aware. Her eyes won't ever tell."
What's more, once more: "Assuming that I had enough cash, I'd request that Jane wed me. Be that as it may, I can't pay for Huyler's and matinée tickets. What's more, at any rate, I'm certain she wouldn't have me. Not without skipping a beat. We're made for one another okay. Also, sometime in the future, on the off chance that she doesn't have any acquaintance with it, I'll make her."
There were spring days with Jane. "Hmm, however it's great to be alive. Jane and I strolled down to the glen earlier today. Picked wild blossoms, dogtooth violets, hepatica, anemones; and we sang — with no one to hear us. I let out my voice — in the Toreador's tune, and Jane stayed

there and looked and tuned in, and said when I had gotten done, 'It resembles the show, Evans.' I accept she implied it, and she didn't need me to stop.... I felt pretty fine to have her there, preferring it.... Goodness, she's a dear. I needed to tell her, however I didn't."

Pre-winter came: "Jane and I went to-day to assemble fox grapes. Mother is making jam as is Jane. The plants were an extraordinary knot. Close in among them we appeared to be 1,000 miles from the world. Jane made herself a wreath of grape leaves, and seemed to be a sprite of the forest. I told her so and she looked at me with those extraordinary dark eyes of hers and said, 'Evans, when the divine beings were youthful they probably lived this way — with grapes for their food, and the birds to sing for them, and the little wild things of the wood for organization. It would be radiant, wouldn't it?' She's an eccentric youngster. An existence with her wouldn't be uninteresting. She's so serious herself."

"We discussed the conflict. I told her I ought to go assuming France required me. I won't hold on until this nation gets into it. We owe an obligation to France...."

He halted there, and shut the book. He didn't want to peruse farther. Gracious, his obligation to France had been paid. Furthermore, after that day with Jane among the tangled plants things had moved quicker — and quicker.

He would have rather not considered it....

## Part XII

## THE ICE PALACE

The night wrap which Jane wore with her old white chiffon was of a splendid Madonna blue with a dark fur collar. Jane, as has been said, cherished clear tones, and when she colored shabby things she delivered them wonderfully to the eye and enormously pleasant.

The primary impact on Frederick Towne of her weaved clogged pore over the fur collar was captivating. The fact that he found her decrepitude makes it simply later. That underlying impression had, nonetheless, shown him how cash could help her.

Frederick's home was where cleaned floors appeared to break down in pools of brilliant light, where a fantastic flight of stairs hinted at galleries, where the roofs were staggeringly high, the vistas unquestionably remote. Frederick, coming towards her through those pools of brilliant light — blonde, enormous and grinning, brought a quick memory of another blonde and gallant figure, not in night garments — but rather in silver defensive layer — "Pious devotee sei bedankt, mein lieber Schwan," Lohengrin! That was all there was to it.

"A fat Lohengrin," she changed, noxiously.

Ignorant about this overwhelming evaluation, Frederick invited her with the quality of a Cophetua. He was unaware of his disposition of loftiness. He was quite drawn in, however he knew, obviously, that his advantage in her eventually was something extraordinary for the young lady. What's more, he was intrigued. Something strange had happened to him — a thing which conflicted with every one of his hypotheses, separated the rationale of his past contentions. He had gone gaga for little Jane Barnes, from the beginning if it's all the same to you — like an unrefined kid. What's more, he needed her for his significant other. It was what was going on. There had been such countless ladies he could have hitched. Lovelier ladies than Jane, wittier, more recognized, more extravagant — of more guaranteed social standing. He might have had the pick of them, at this point not one of them had he needed. Here was little Jane Barnes, weaved hair, innocent, slim, curious in her modest garments, and he could see no other person at the top of his table, no other person close by in the huge vehicle, no other person to share the captivating long periods of special night, and the existence which was to follow.

He had consistently had his own specific manner, and he planned to have it now. Edith had, obviously, obstructed him in certain things, and she was still in his hands. However the matter would, without uncertainty, right itself. There were other qualified admirers; it was not to be assumed that a stunner and a beneficiary would stay long unwed.

Furthermore, he would set himself to the charm of Jane. The end was, obviously, unavoidable. However, Jane wouldn't fall into his arms at the principal's word. Her demeanor towards him was totally unoriginal. She had no blushes, no little coquettish stunts. She was just about as cool as some beautiful nursery bloom with the morning dew upon it. Be that as it may, he liked she could fire.

Thus when youthful Baldwin had called of Edith's arrangements, there had jumped into Towne's brain the acknowledgment of his chance. He would see Jane among his family divine beings. Also, he would see her alone. He had sent Briggs so as to have her there before the others showed up.

Also, presently Fate had played further into his hands. "I've had one more message from Edith," he told her; "we'll need to have supper without them. The haze got them south of Alexandria, and they went into a trench. They will eat at the closest inn while the vehicle is being repaired."

"Baldy's vehicle generally breaks at mental minutes," said Jane. "In the event that it hadn't separated on the extension, he could never have tracked down your niece."

"What's more, I could never have known you" — he was grinning at her. "Who might at any point have trusted that such a lot held tight to pretty much nothing."

What's more, presently Waldron, the steward, reported supper — and Jane going into the lounge area felt overshadowed by the Gargantuan tables, the high-upheld ministerial seats, the tall silver candles with their orange candles.

"Your variety," Towne told her. "You see I recollected your weaving — — "
"I'm obsessed with splendid fleeces," said Jane; "some time or another I will open a shop and sell them."
However, he realized that she wouldn't open a shop. "You resembled some wonderful bird, — an oriole, maybe, with your orange and dark."
"I color things," said Jane, honestly; "you ought to see a portion of my garments when they emerge. Joseph's jacket isn't in it."
Frederick enjoyed her candor. He knew individuals who might have been embarrassed to concede their neediness before Waldron and the servants. To Jane, workers had neither eyes nor ears — in that she showed her typicality. Individuals who had never been served were unsure.
"The following time you see this dress," Jane was saying, "it will be pretty much as blue as my jacket. What's more, I'll have a support of copper lace, and Baldy will paint my shoes with copper paint."
She grinned at him with her jawline shifted in her bird-like way. She was truly having a great time. She was excited and captivated by the magnificence of her environmental factors, and slowly Frederick started to take on something of interest. Against his own experience, he displayed his best. Without a single word of disgusting bootlicking, he caused little Jane to feel that she was a respected visitor. He talked very well, and however she was distant from everyone else with him put her totally at her simplicity.

The food was tasty. There had been a divine canape, an eminent soup, fish that were pale pink and covered in tartar sauce.
"He is really great," Jane let herself know out of her preeminent substance, as Waldron passed squabs with a royal flair. She alluded obviously to Towne and not to Waldron but rather, recollecting her own old Sophy's deficiencies, she set aside the opportunity, additionally, to praise to herself the head servant's expertness.
After supper they sat in the extraordinary drawing-room — an ominous spot — with low-hung gem light fixtures — pale mats — pale walls — with one corner recovered from the overall coldness by a chimney of yellow Italian marble, and an immense screen of peacock feathers in a mahogany outline.
"I call this room the Ice Palace," Frederick told her. "Mother outfitted it in the mid eighties — and she could never transform it. Furthermore, presently I prefer not to have it unique. I warmed this corner with the chimney and the screen. Edith generally sits in the library on the opposite side of the corridor, yet Mother and I had our espresso here, and I like to proceed with the old custom."
Jane's eyes opened wide. "Don't you and your niece drink your espresso together?"
"Normally, yet there have been times," he chuckled as he said it, "when every one of us has reclined on across from sides of the corridor in forlorn state."

Jane snickered as well. "Baldy and I do things like that."
"What's more, presently," he said, "we can discuss Edith. I guess I'll need to kill the fatted calf. Your sibling said that."
"That sounds like Baldy."
"Right? Indeed, he let me know what concluded her was a few companions who emerged and saw her in the lounge area. She's been constantly with Martha, her mom's old cook, whose spouse keeps a country inn past Alexandria. Furthermore, Adelaide Laramore and Eloise Harper and several men were eating there. I'm sorry it worked out. Eloise is a customary local proclaimer. She'll tell the world."
He beat his clench hand against the arm of his seat. "I prefer not to have the thing in the papers."
"It will before long fade away," said Jane, "when she gets back home."
"I would love to have her. However, I don't exactly see the reason why I am killing the fatted calf. She won't act at all like a reckless person."
"For what reason would it be a good idea for you to mind how she acts? You need her back. Isn't that excessive?"
He loved her fresh presence of mind. Her daring articulation of assessment. The majority of the ladies he knew were apprehensive not to concur with him. That was the issue with Adelaide. She inclined to him generally like a lily, beguiling, ladylike, delicate as milk. Yet, Jane didn't incline. She was, he told himself, a cup of remedy held to

his lips. He drank figuratively speaking of her childhood.

They completed their espresso and he smoked a stogie. Edith and Baldy called that the thing was more serious than they had expected. Maybe he would be wise to send Briggs.

"So that implies I will have you to myself for an hour longer," Frederick told Jane. "I truly want to believe that you are as cheerful as I am."

"I'm making some happy memories. I feel like Cinderella at the ball."

He giggled at that. "You're an invigorating youngster, Jane." He had until recently never called her by her most memorable name.

"Am I? In any case, I'm not a kid. I'm basically ancient."

"Not in years."

"In shrewdness. I know how to earn enough to get by, and how to arrange feasts, and how to design my own dresses, and a ton of things that your Edith doesn't need to ponder."

"But then you are cheerful."

"I'll say I am."

He chuckled yet didn't proceed with the subject. "I've a somewhat brilliant assortment of hoops. Might you want to check them out? Eccentric prevailing fashion, right? Yet, I've gotten them all over."

"Why hoops?"

"Different things are ordinary — clasps, pieces of jewelry, headdresses. Yet, there's sentiment in the gems that ladies have worn in their ears. You'll see."

He went into one more space and brought back a plate. It was fixed with velvet and the studs were set up on small pads. It was a remarkable showcase. Appearances from old Rome, oak seeds of human hair in the terrible taste of the sixties — vagabond circles of gold — coral roses in sensitive worried wreaths — old French gems — rubies, emeralds, sapphires, and seed pearls, bigger pearls set alone to show their excellence, and a shining cluster of current things, jewels in platinum — long pendants of jade and fly — opals trickling like fluid fire along slim chains.

She loomed over them.

"Which do you like best?" he inquired. "The pearls?"

He was dicey. "Not the white ones. These — — " he got a couple of sapphires set in seed pearls — rather boorish things that draped down for an inch or more. "They'll suit your style. Have you at any point worn studs?"

"No."

"Attempt them."

He assisted her with changing them — and his hand contacted her smooth warm cheek. He was aware of her closeness, yet offered no hint.

There was a little mirror over the shelf. "Take a gander at yourself," he said.

She shifted her head with the goal that the gems shook. The blue lights of the stones made her skin glowing.

Frederick overviewed her fundamentally. "You should have a more refined outfit. Silver brocade with a wisp of a train."

"It transforms me, right? I don't know that I like them."

"Indeed I do. Edith has for practically forever needed those studs. Be that as it may, I won't allow her to have them. I'm saving them for — my significant other."

"You should have spouses to wear them — like Solomon."

"Do you imply that you are suggesting it?"

"Obviously not. Just a single lady could never at any point wear them all, right?"

"She may." Again he was satisfied by her absence of reluctance. What a delight she was after Adelaide.

As though the name had brought her, a voice talked from the entryway. "I couldn't allow Waldron to report me, Ricky; may I come in?"

She halted as she saw Jane.

"Gracious, no doubt about it?"

"This is Miss Barnes, Adelaide. I think you met her sibling to-day at lunch get-together. Edith called out that you and Eloise had seen her."

"That is the very thing I came to fruition, to caution you. Eloise has the columnists following right after her. She'll be over in a moment. Be that as it may, the damage will be finished, I am apprehensive, before you can stop her."

"Goodness, I've surrendered. Edith's returning to-night. Miss Barnes' sibling is bringing her."

"Truly?" Adelaide Laramore was evaluating Jane. A ratty kid. From the edge she had a snapshot of envy. However, the second was past. Frederick was very critical. He revered excellence and this Barnes kid was not delightful.

What Mrs. Laramore neglected to see was that Jane's magnificence was of an extremely exceptional kind. It was not normalized. It was not marceled and cold-creamed, and rouged and powdered. In any case, it had to do with illuminated eyes, with youth and a nonconformist. Also, it was these things in her which had drawn in Frederick.

Jane was detaching the studs. "Might it be said that they are great, Mrs. Laramore?"

"The sapphires?" Mrs. Laramore plunked down on the lounge chair. Her night wrap slipped back, showing her white neck. Her fair hair was cleared up from her temple. She had a brooding look, with pink cheeks and penciled eyebrows. She resembled a picture on porcelain, and she knew it, and stressed the impact. "The sapphires? Indeed. They're the decision of the part."

She proceeded to discuss Eloise.

"She is just sad. She has told the most furious stories and every one of the papers have sent men out to the Inn."

"Indeed, they got away. They began early and have been hung up at Alexandria."

"Eloise and Benny and the Captain feasted with me. She was calling all the while when I left. I told her that I didn't endorse it, and that I ought to come straight finished and tell you. Yet, she snickered and said she couldn't have cared less. That she thought it was extraordinary tomfoolery and that you were a decent game."

"I shan't see her," right away; "she should have better sense than that.

Setting correspondents on Edith like a bunch of wolves."
"I told her how you would feel," Adelaide repeated.
"I ought to see her if I were in your shoes, Mr. Towne," said a fresh, youthful voice.
Adelaide turned with a pant. With her slippered feet crossed before her, Jane seemed to be a kid. Interestingly Mrs. Laramore got a decent perspective on those real to life dim eyes. They strangely affected her. Eyes like that were generally exceptional. Valiant. The young lady was not scared of Frederick. She was not scared of anybody.
"For what reason would it be advisable for me to see her?" Frederick requested.
"Could it simply add to her feeling of acting in the event that you don't? Also, for what reason would it be a good idea for you to mind? Your niece is returning home. Also, that is its finish."
"You mean," Frederick requested, "that I am to steal it away with air?"
Jane gestured. "Make satire of it rather than misfortune."
Adelaide getting out of her wrap was uncovered as exquisite and recognized in silver and dark.
"May I have a cigarette, Ricky, to settle my nerves? Eloise is colossally disturbing." Adelaide was mournful.
Jane watched her with enthusiastic interest. The ladies she knew didn't smoke. Baldy's flappers did, however they were strange and of another age. Mrs. Laramore was mature enough to be Jane's mom, and Jane had an

inclination ... that moms ... shouldn't smoke....

Be that as it may, nonetheless, Adelaide Laramore and her intriguing ways were entertaining. She had a fragile and counterfeit look, similar to the Manchu woman in the Museum, or something in wax.

Jane was brought back from her contemplation by the crazy entry of Eloise and the two men.

"I realized Adelaide was telling stories."

"I let you know I was coming, Eloise."

Eloise gazed at Jane when Frederick introduced her. "You seem to be your sibling. Twins?"

"No." Jane concluded that she loved Miss Harper better than she did Mrs. Laramore — which wasn't saying — much....

"The journalists are en route to Alexandria — full cry." Eloise all in emerald green, with her red hair in an exemplary hairstyle, resembled some brilliant witch, jubilant of malevolence. "You mustn't reprove me, Frederick. It was frightfully energizing to tell them, and I love energy."

"They aren't there."

"Where could they be?"

Frederick recited composedly, "We three know ... in any case, we won't ever tell...."

"Adelaide will, when I get her alone."

"I will not."

"Then Miss Barnes will. Do you have any idea about how youthful you look, Miss Barnes? I feel as though you'd let me know anything for a stick of treats."

They thundered at that. Also, Jane said, "No one caused me to do anything I would have rather not done."

What's more, presently Benny and the Captain took a gander at her, and looked once more. What a voice the kid had, and eyes!

Eloise, on the love seat, embraced her knees and reviewed her gold shoes. "They are placing my image in the paper and Adelaide's. They saw one directly in front of me — — "

Mrs. Laramore shouted out, "Benny, for what reason did you let her make it happen?" and there was an extraordinary commotion — in which Eloise could heard say:

"Furthermore, they will have an image of the Inn, and one of your siblings in the event that they can get it, Miss Barnes."

Jane started to feel awkward. She was, she told herself, as awkward as a feline in a zoo. These ladies and these men helped her in some way to remember the extraordinary smooth creatures who growled at one another in the Rock Creek confines. Frederick didn't growl. Yet, she had an inclination he may in the event that Eloise kept at him significantly longer.

It was amidst the commotion that Edith entered. She strolled in among them as composedly as she had confronted them at the Inn.

"Hi," she said, "you sound like a jazz band." She went straight up to Frederick and kissed him. "I guess Eloise is yelling the information to the world." She wrapped her hand up his arm. "There are in excess of 1,000,000 correspondents outside. Mr.

Barnes is keeping them under control."
"Where did they track you down?"
"Known about us, I assume, at the Alexandria inn. We didn't understand it until we arrived here, and afterward they heaped out and started to seek clarification on some pressing issues."
Frederick lifted her hand from his arm. "I'll proceed to send them away."
Eloise hopped up. "I'll go with you."
And afterward Frederick growled, "Remain here."
In any case, neither of them went, for Baldy entered, head positioned, eyes land — Jane knew the signs.
"They've gone," he said. "I let you know I'd dispose of them, Miss Towne."
He gestured to them all. Totally at his simplicity, lifted above them generally by the worship of his mind-set. Better, Jane told herself, than any of them — his delightful youth against their reality exhaustion.
Edith was grinning at Jane. "I knew you without a moment's delay. You resemble your sibling."
They were indistinguishable. A striking pair as they stood together. "It is a direct result of Mr. Barnes and his sister that we reached out to Edith," Frederick made sense of. He had recaptured his amicable way.
"Gracious, truly." Adelaide realizes that she and her companions should go without a moment's delay. Edith looked drained, and Eloise at minutes like this was unthinkable. In any case, she would have rather not leave any other person in the field. "Might I at any point give you a lift?" she asked

Jane, pleasantly, "you and your sibling."
However, it was Frederick who replied. "Miss Barnes lives in Sherwood Park. Briggs will take her out."
So Adelaide disappeared, and Eloise and the two men, and Edith went to her uncle and said, "Please accept my apologies."
Her face was white and her eyes were sparkling, and out of nowhere she reached up her arms and put them about his neck and cried as though her heart would break.
And afterward, and not up to that point, little Jane realizes that Edith dislikes one of the creatures at the Zoo.

## Part XIII

## JANE POURS TEA

In Jane's next letter to Judy she told her how the night with the Townes had finished.
"Edith demanded that I ought to remain throughout the evening. She's an ideal dear, so totally and completely dazzling, but so human. She and her uncle can't check out things from a similar point. Furthermore, they are both to fault. Anything sets them off, — you ought to have seen them — like individuals in a play.
"I rested in the extra room — and all things considered, I lay awake a portion of the late evening taking a gander at it, and respecting myself in one of Edith's nighties! I never saw such underthings, Judy! For a princess! Her room is completely rose and silver and ivory, and the room I

stayed in is in light yellow — with a covering to my bed of gold brocade.
"Edith and I ate together. Everything was raised on a plate and set in her little living room, and we wore trim covers and breakfast covers, and looked — standout! Edith is the most gorgeous individual — like one of the Viking ladies — with her hair in thick fair plaits. I told her that, and she chuckled. 'What a couple of writers you are,' she said, 'you and your sibling.'
"Hearing her laugh was great. She cried frightfully the prior night. Returning was hard for her — and afterward Mr. Towne drove her up the wall. The two of them believed me should remain, and Baldy remained, as well, and I realized his head knocked the mists. Furthermore, toward the beginning of today en route to the workplace, he purchased a lot of heliotrope for Edith and sent it to her.
"The issue with Edith is that her life hasn't been genuine, Judy. Not in the manner that your life and mine and Baldy's is genuine. She has never had any work to do, and nothing has at any point relied on her. Think about it. There's no great explanation for why she can't remain in bed the entire day in the event that she needs to. Furthermore, she can delight any state of mind existing apart from everything else. The result is that a fraction of the time she is worn solid out. She says that was the explanation she became drawn into Delafield Simms. Anything for a change.

"Maybe she and I would have been horrendously amicable. She let me know that she needs me for a companion. That Eloise Harper and her sort are horrendous to her after the things that have occurred.
"To-morrow evening she and her uncle are getting over here to have tea, and I will have the Follettes over. Mrs. Follette will cherish it. Be that as it may, Evans will not. He could do without Mr. Towne.
"What's more, presently, my dearest-dear, I am stressed over that clue in your last letter that you are not great. Deal with yourself, and recall that I have just a single valuable sister, and the youngsters have just a single mother. We really want you in our young lives, and you mustn't buckle down."
At the point when she had composed the last line, Jane stood by at her work area. She was considering Evans. She hadn't seen him for three days. Not since Sunday night has she gone to the Townes. That evening in the haze had dazzled her peculiarly. She had felt for Evans something that didn't have anything to do with appreciation for him nor regard nor engagement. His shortcoming had attracted her to him, as a mother may be attracted to a kid. His battle was, she felt, something which she should share. Not as his better half! No.... That sort of adoration was unique. If by some stroke of good luck he would let her be his younger sibling, Jane. He had not even hit her up. At the point when she had welcomed him and his mom to tea with the Townes,

Mrs. Follette had replied, and had acknowledged the two of them. Evans, she expressed, was in Washington, and would be out on the late train. When he showed up in front of the others on the evening of her tea, Jane said, "Where have you been? Do you realize it has been four days since we've seen one another?"

"Is it safe to say that you weren't happy to dispose of me? I've considered you consistently." He dropped into a seat close to her.

She was looking at him with vivacious interest. "How decent you look."

"New suit. Like it?"

"Indeed. Furthermore, you go about as though someone had left you 1,000,000 bucks."

"Wish he had. I purchased this outfit with the first release 'Alice in Wonderland,'" he giggled and made sense of it. "I've been disposing of a portion of our intriguing books. I feel plutocratic as a result. 500 bucks, if you don't mind, for that old Hogarth, with the blistering Ruskin engraving. Furthermore, I will open an office, Jane."

"In Washington?"

"On Connecticut Avenue. Same structure, same room, where I began."

"Evans, how wonderful!"

"Indeed. You did it, Jane."

"I? How?"

"The evening of the haze. I never acknowledged before what a mobile stick I've been — resting on you. Hence you're the Lady of the Lantern. It will not be so exhausting."

He was grinning at her, and she grinned back. However peculiarly and

conflictingly, she felt as though in changing his mentality towards her, he had denied her of some honor. "I wouldn't fret being a mobile stick."
"All things considered, I disapproved. After this I'll walk alone. Furthermore, I will really buckle down, and play around a little. Will you have tea with me to-morrow, Jane? At the Willard? To commend my most memorable wobbling advances."
She concurred, enthusiastically. "It will resemble bygone eras."
"Short a ton, old woman."
That was the manner in which he had conversed with her quite a while back. The mournful note was no more.
"Take the three-thirty train and I'll meet you. I'll pay for the taxi with what's left of 'Alice.'"
"Try not to be excessively extreme."
"Nothing is excessively great for you, Jane. I can't express it as I need to say it, however you won't ever understand what you appeared to me on Sunday as you got through the fog."
His voice shook a bit, however he recuperated himself in a second.
"Here come the Townes." He rose as Edith entered with youthful Baldwin. After that Evans took cues from Baldy as a gadget of neighborliness. Both of them passed cups, passed slim bread and butter, passed little cakes, passed lemon and cream and sugar, flung conversational balls as light as plumes up high, were, as Baldy would have communicated it, "the bubbling energy source everyone crowds around."
"Something probably has gone to Casabianca's head," Frederick Towne

commented to Jane. "Have you at any point seen him like this?"
"Quite a while back. He was massively appealing."
"Do you track down him alluring now?" with a bit of disturbance.
"I track down him — magnificent" — her tone was rebellious — "and I've known him for my entire life."
"Assuming you had known me for your entire life could you call me brilliant?"
She checked out at him from behind her bulwarks of silver. "How would I be aware? Individuals need to show off their abilities."
Dr. Hallam had driven Mrs. Follette over. He seldom did social tricks, yet he preferred Jane. Furthermore, he had been intrigued enough with regards to Evans to need to see him in his new role.
Walking around to the coffee table, he knew immediately of a circumstance which could make for parody, or without a doubt for misfortune. It was apparent that Towne was quite drawn to little Jane Barnes. Assuming Jane responded, what of youthful Follette? Hallam knew Towne, and himself a single man of very another sort, without vanity where ladies were concerned, he had a sensation of hatred for a man whose standing was connected with a long queue of much-discussed women. What's more, presently little Jane was the supreme sovereign. He could have done without the possibility of her childhood, and Towne's late forties.
"I saw Mrs. Laramore yesterday," he said, suddenly, "wonderful as could be — — "

"Indeed, obviously." Towne wanted Hallam to not discuss Adelaide. He wanted that all of the others would disappear and abandon him with Jane.

"Mrs. Laramore," said Jane suddenly, "makes me consider the woman of Shalott. I don't have the foggiest idea why. Yet, I do. I have actually never seen such a wonderful lady. Yet, she doesn't appear to be genuine. I have an inclination that in the event that anything hit her, she'd break like china."

They giggled at her, and Edith said, "Adelaide won't ever break. She'll dissolve. She's just about as delicate as wax." Then categorizing Mrs. Laramore for additional imperative matters. "Uncle Fred, I am going out to Baldy's studio; he's painting Jane."

Frederick was intrigued. "Her picture?"

"No. A sketch for a magazine contest," Baldy made sense of.

"May I see it?"

Baldy, longing for isolation and Edith, gave hesitant assent. "Come on, everyone."

So everyone, including Dr. Hallam and Mrs. Follette, advanced toward the carport.

Edith and youthful Baldwin showed up first. "Furthermore, this is where you work," she said, delicately.

"Indeed. Look here, will you stay here with the goal that I can behold you? I've longed for you in that seat — in an exemplary outfit. Do you have any idea that you were made for a goddess?"

"I realize that you are a heartfelt kid."

However as she sat in the nursery seat which he had changed into a high position for her by tossing a mat over it and setting it up over the others on a little stage, she moaned a bit.
Here in this little room he spent his extra minutes. He glanced out through that little square window on the downpours and snow, and the youthful green of the spring — and he attempted to paint his fantasies, yet was kept down since he was fastened to the kitchen of a Government work. Also, in the event that he was not fastened, what could he not do? On the off chance that somebody waved a wand and set him free? Furthermore, in the event that the somebody who waved a wand cherished him? Motivated him? Might he not provide for anything sometime a work of art? All things considered, no difference either way. She wound up excited with the idea. To be a light and light the way!
"How old are you?" she asked him.
"25."
"I don't trust it. I'm 22, and I feel 1,000 years more seasoned than you."
"You will continuously be — imperishable."
She snickered. "How old is Jane?"
"Twenty. However, individuals take us for twins."
"She doesn't look at it and neither do you."
The others came in and Edith returned to her viewpoints. He wasn't excessively youthful. She was happy about that....
The sketch of Jane was on an easel. There she stood, a slim figure in her

lilac gown — bounced dark hair, illuminated eyes — the lifted bushel with its weight of gold and purple and green!

Towne remained back and checked it out. Jane next to him said, "That is a portion of the organic product you sent."

"Truly?" Frederick had no eyes for everything except Jane, in her lilac gown. Jove, however the kid had gotten the soul of her!

He went to Baldy. "It is generally surprising. What's more, I need it."

"Sorry," said Baldy, freshly. "I'm sending it off to-morrow."

"How much is the award?"

"2,000 bucks."

"I will compose a check for that sum in the event that you will allow me to have this."

"I'm apprehensive I can't, Mr. Towne."

"Same difference either way."

"All things considered, I feel as such about it. It isn't valued at 2,000 bucks. Yet, assuming I win the award it could merit that to the magazine — the promoting what not."

"Isn't that quibbling?"

"Maybe, yet it's the manner in which I feel."

"Yet, on the off chance that you don't win the award you will not have anything."

"No."

"Furthermore, you'll be out 2,000 bucks." The lion in the Zoo was growling.

Or more him, breathing an upper air, was this youthful falcon. "I'll love to give the sketch to you assuming it returns," said Baldy, coolly, "yet I rather figure it will stick."

It was, as it were, a horrible second for Towne. There was a youthful Baldwin sitting on the edge of the table, swinging a leg, smooth, rebellious. What's more, Edith giggling in her sleeve. Frederick realized that she was chuckling. He was essentially as red as a turkey rooster.

It was Jane who saved him from blood vessel breakage. She was actually unreasonably glad for Baldy, however she knew the risks of his state of mind. Also, she had her obligations as leader.

"Baldy needs to see himself on the newsstands," she said, soothingly; "don't deny him of that delight, Mr. Towne."

"Nothing of the sort, Jane," shouted her sibling.

"Baldy, I won't fight with you before individuals. We should hold that delight until we are distant from everyone else."

"I'm not quarreling."

Jane held up a fighting hand.

"Goodness, we should take off from him, Mr. Towne. At the point when he starts like that, there's no limit to it."

She conveyed Frederick back to the house, and Evans, caring for them, expressed noxiously to Hallam, "Old Midas got his that time."

Dr. Hallam laughed. "You don't abhor him, isn't that right? Evans, don't allow him to have Jane. He isn't worth the effort."

"Nor am I," said Evans. "Yet, I would know better how to satisfy her."

Yet again back in the splendid minimal family room, Towne told Jane, "May I have one more cup of tea?"
"It's a virus."
"I couldn't care less. I like to see you pour it with your beautiful hands."
She spread her hands out on the sparkling mahogany of the coffee table. "Is it true that they are wonderful? No one at any point told me."
His hand went over hers. "The loveliest on the planet."
She stayed there in a second's short breath. Then, at that point, she drew her hands away. Contacted a little ringer. "I'll have Sophy present to us some boiling water."
Sophy went back and forth. Jane poured hot tea with flushed cheeks. He took the cup when she gave it to him. "Dear kid, you're not kidding?"
"I'm not a kid, Mr. Towne." Her lashes were brought down, her cheeks flushed.
He put his cup down and inclined towards her. "You are in excess of a kid to me — a dearest lady. Jane, you shouldn't need to fear me.... I need you for my better half!"
Her flabbergasted eyes met his. "Yet, we haven't known one another for seven days."
"I was unable to cherish you more in the event that I had known you for 1,000 years."
"Mr. Towne — please." He was extremely near her.
"Kiss me, Jane."
She held her slim figure away from him. "You should not."
"I should."

"No, really.... Please," she was breathing rapidly. "Please." She was on her feet, the coffee table between them.
He saw his mix-up. "Pardon me."
Her open eyes met his. "Mr. Towne, could you have behaved this way ... with Edith's companions?"
Edith's companions! The kid's honesty! Adelaide's kisses went for pretty much nothing. Eloise honestly offered hers. Edith was saved by just some internal elegance.
"Jane, they are not worth your little finger. I put you most importantly. On a platform. Truly. What's more, I believe that you should wed me."
"Yet, I don't adore you."
"I'll make you. I have all that to give you."
Had he? What of Robin Hood and Galahad? What of youth and youth's dauntlessness, high purposes, flaring dreams?
She felt something of this subliminally. In any case, she could never have been a female animal had she not felt the bootlicking of his interest.
"Jane, I'll make life a fantasy. We'll travel all over. Sail bizarre oceans. Couldn't you adore it — that large number of nations you have never seen — and simply both of us? And every one of the spots you have found out about? Furthermore, when we return home I'll fabricate you a house — any place you express — with an extraordinary nursery."
He was persuasive, and the things he guaranteed were woven into the woof of all her juvenile imaginings.

"I should not tune in," she said, tremblingly.
Yet, he realized that she had tuned in. He was adequately insightful to leave it — there.
He rose as he heard the others returning. "Will you ride with me to-morrow evening? Try not to fear me. I'll vow to be great."
"Sorry. I'm going to have tea with Evans."
"Might you at any point break the commitment?"
"I won't break my commitment." The rooster of her head was like Baldy's.
"Gracious, you don't. Sometimes you'll break them for me." But he preferred her autonomy. It guaranteed a lot of that sounds invigorating. What's more, he would constantly be the Conqueror. He jumped at the chance to feel that he would be — the Conqueror.
So he disappeared secure in the prospect of Jane's last acquiescence. There was everything in it for her, and the kid should see it. Her wavering was regular. She proved unable, obviously, to come at the main law breaker of his finger. Be that as it may, she would come.

## Section XIV

## A TELEGRAM

"Janey — — !"
"Indeed, Baldy." Jane sat up in bed, dreams still in her eyes. She had been late in getting to rest. There had been such a great amount to consider — Frederick Towne's proposition — the frightening change in Evans — —
"It's a wire. Open the entryway, dear."
She got up to speed her robe and folded it over her. "A wire?" She was

with him now in the lobby. "Baldy, is it Judy?"
"Indeed. She's evil. Inquires as to whether you can come on and take care of the youngsters."
"Obviously." She influenced me a bit. "Clutch me a moment, Baldy. It blows my mind."
"You mustn't be terrified, old young lady."
"I'll be good in ... a minute...."
His arms were tight about her. "Maybe I ought to go, as well, Janey."
"However, you can't. I'll prepare things and ride in with you for the first part of the day. I'll pack my trunk assuming you'll bring it down from the storage room. I can rest on the train to-morrow."
Furthermore, when he had taken it she made him hit the hay. The house was extremely still. Merrymaid, waked by the uncommon fervor, came up-steps and sat, round-peered toward, by Jane, watching her overlap her insufficient closet and murmuring a melody of relief. Jane figured out an opportunity sometimes to pause and smooth the smooth head, and when she got Merrymaid in her arms, and the tears trickled on the old feline's fur.
Philomel sang promptly the following morning. It was Baldy who made the espresso, and who called Sophy and the Follettes. Mrs. Follette demanded that Baldy ought to remain at Castle Manor in Jane's nonappearance. "It will do Evans great, and we'd very much want to have him."
So that was settled. Furthermore, Evans came over while the youngsters were eating breakfast.

"Try not to stress over anything," he said. "Baldy and I will care for the chickens — and take the little felines over to Castle Manor. I'll wrap them all in cotton fleece as opposed to having anything happen to them. Worry, don't either."

What she stressed over was Judy. "She let me know in one of her letters that she wasn't well."

Baldy went to bring his vehicle around, and Evans remained with his hand on the rear of Jane's seat, peering down at her. "You'll keep in touch with me, Jane?"

"Goodness, obviously."

He moved his hand from the seat back to her shoulder. "Dear young lady, in the event that my bumbling petitions to God will help you any — you'll have them."

She turned in her seat and gazed toward him. She was unable to talk. Yet again their eyes met, and Jane had that winded feeling of vacillating wings inside her that lifted to the sun.

Then Baldy was back, and the sacks were prepared, and there was only that last hand-catch. "God favor you, Jane...."

Frederick Towne was on the train. He had been overwhelmed at the insight about Jane's flight. "Do you imply that you will remain endlessly?" he had asked over the wire.

"I will remain however long Judy needs me."

Frederick had blossoms for her, books and a major box of desserts.

Individuals in the Pullman gazed at Jane amidst all her radiance. They gazed as well, at Towne, and at

Briggs, who hurried in without a second to spare with additional books from Brentano.

Edith and Baldy were on the stage. Edith had caught Towne. So Frederick, alone with Jane, said, "I maintain that you should consider the things we discussed yesterday — — "

"Please, not currently. Gracious, I'm apprehensive — — "

"Of me? You mustn't be."

"Not of you — of everything — Life."

He grasped her hand and held it. "Is there something else I can get done for you? All that I have is — yours, you know — assuming you need it."

He needed to leave her then, at that point, with a last close catch of the hand. She saw him by and by remaining adjacent to Baldy on the station stage — the focal point of the eyes of everyone — the incomparable Frederick Towne!

As the city got away and she rested her head up against the pads and watched out at the flying fields — it appeared to be something breathtaking that a man like Towne ought to have laid his fortune at her feet. However she had barely any clue of elation. She loved the things he brought to the table — longed for them — however she didn't need him next to her.

In her distress her heart went to the kid who had staggered over the words, "In the event that my bungling petitions to heaven will help you — — "

She wound up wailing — the main tears she had shed since the appearance of the wire.

At the point when she arrived in Chicago, her brother by marriage, Bob Heming, met her. "Judy's standing her ground," he said, as he kissed her. "It was no great closure for you to come, Janey."

"Are you a medical caretaker?"

"Two. Day attendant and night nurture. What's more, a servant. Judy is almost hysterical about the cost. It isn't great for her, either, to stress. That is a portion of the difficulty. I attempted to cause her to find support, yet she wouldn't. Yet, I fault myself for not demanding it."

"Try not to fault yourself, Bob. Judy wouldn't. She let me know she could get along. Furthermore, when Judy concludes a thing, nobody can change her."

"All things considered, times have been hard. What's more, business is terrible. What's more, Judy knew it. She's a decent game."

They were in a taxi, so when attacks Heming's eyes, he put forth no attempt to disguise them.

"I'm just pretty much holding nothing back. You can't comprehend the amount it means to me to have you here."

"What's more, now that I am here," said Jane, with a bravery brought into the world of his need for her, "things will be better."

The loft was essentially outfitted and bore the stamp of Judy's great taste. A companion had taken the kids out to ride, so the rooms were extremely tranquil as Jane went through them. Judy in bed was white and slight, and Jane needed to sob over her, yet she

didn't. "You favored an old young lady," she said, "you will move well immediately."
"The specialist figures I might have an activity. That is the reason I believed I should wire you." Judy was restless. "I was unable to leave the children with outsiders. Furthermore, it was critical to such an extent that Bob ought to be at his work."
"Obviously," said Jane; "how about anything that has made me stay away?"
Judy gave a speedy moan of help. How grand to have Janey! Furthermore, what a dear she was with her demeanor of overcoming the world. Jane had forever been that way — with that overcoming air. It cheered one just to check her out.
The children, showing up as of now in a romping condition of energy over the coming of Auntie Jane, showed themselves great and loving.
"Junior," said Jane, "would you say you are happy I'm here?"
"Did you bring me anything?"
"Something — superb — — "
"What?"
She opened her pack, and delivered Towne's case of desserts. "May I give him a chocolate, Judy?"
"One minimal one, and simply a preference for children. Jane, where did you get that stunning box?"
"Frederick Towne."
"Truly? My dear, your letters have been hugely fascinating. Haven't they, Bob?"
Her significant other gestured. He was perched by the bedside holding her

hand. "Towne's a quite enormous man."
In a snapshot of vaingloriousness, Jane needed to share with them, "What is your take of your odd one out? Mr. Towne maintains that she should be his significant other." But obviously she didn't. Not before Bob. She'd tell Judy, later, obviously.
The attendant came in then, at that point, and Jane went with Bob and the children to the lounge area.
Junior over his bread and milk was honestly basic. "I didn't think you'd be so old. Mother said you'd play with me."
"I can play marvelous games, Junior."
"Could you? What kind?"
"Indeed, there's one about a feline. Furthermore, I'm the large feline and you're the little feline — and I am Merrymaid."
"What is the little feline's name?"
"We'll need to see as one. We can't simply call him Kitty, can we?"
"Indeed, we can. My name's Kitty, and you go by Merrymaid, and — what do we do, Aunt Janey?"
"We drink milk," instantly.
"An' what else?"
"We play with balls — I'll show you after supper."
"I believe that you should show me now."
His dad mediated. "Auntie Janey's worn out. Stand by till she's had her supper."
Junior drank his milk nicely. "I'm a kitty — and you're a feline. How about you drink milk, as well, Aunt Janey?"
Jane grinned at Bob. "Do I need to address every one of his inquiries?"

"Regardless of whether you do, he'll continue to inquire."

However, after supper, Junior nodded off in Jane's arms, having been entertained on a happy eating regimen of "The Three Bears" and "The Little Red Hen."

"They're such marvels, Judy," said Jane, as she returned to her sister.

"Be that as it may, they don't seem to be any of the Barnes."

"No, they're like Bob, with their white skins and fair hair. I believed one of them should have our shading. Do you have any idea how especially wonderful you are becoming, Janey?"

"Judy, I'm not."

"Indeed, you are. What's more, not even one of us thought about it. Thus Mr. Towne needs to wed you?"

"How would you be aware?"

"It is in your eyes, dear, and in the rooster of your head. You and Baldy generally look that way when something exciting happens to you. You can't trick me."

"All things considered, I'm not in adoration with him. So it's as simple as that, Judy."

"Yet, — it's an incredible open door, isn't it, Jane?"

"I guess it is," gradually, "yet I can't exactly see it."

"What difference would it make?"

"Indeed, he's excessively old for a certain thing."

"Just forty — — ? Rich men don't become old. What's more, he could give you everything — everything, Janey." Judy's voice rose a bit. "Jane, you don't have any idea wanting things for those you love and do not have the option to have them. Weave did very well until the downturn in business. Yet, since the children came — I have worked until — all things considered, until maybe I was unable to stand it. Bounce's such a sweetheart. I wouldn't transform anything. I'd wed him over again to-morrow. Yet, I really do know this, that Frederick Towne could make life beautiful for you, and maybe you will not be able to wed a man like that."

"Gracious, don't — don't." It appeared to be awful to Jane to have Judy talk that way, as though life had somehow or another bombed her. Life mustn't fall flat, and it wouldn't on the off chance that one had mental fortitude. Judy was debilitated, and things didn't gaze directly.

"See here, old dear," Jane expressed, "fall asleep and quit pondering how to earn enough to get by. That is my work, and I'll do it."

Also, Judy getting away into invigorating sleep had that vision before her of Jane's young strength — of Jane's gay youthful voice like the sound of silver trumpets....

## Part XV

## EVANS PLAYS THE GAME

Life for Evans Follette after Jane disappeared turned into a kind of game where he played, as he told himself terribly, a Jekyll and Hyde part. Two men fought continually inside him. There was that scarecrow self which breast fed secretive feelings of dread, a withered silver haired self, The Man Who Had Come Back From the War. Furthermore, there was that other, shadowy, subtle, The Boy Who

Once Had Been. Furthermore, it was the Boy who took on steadily shape and substance battling for place with the dim goliath who held frantically to his own.
However the Boy had weapons, confidence and trust. The little journal became a holy book. Inside its pages was detained something that beat with mad wings to be free. Evans, contracting from the program which he constrained himself to follow, was confronted with things like this. "Well, I wish the days were longer. I might want to move through 48 hours at a stretch. Jane is becoming some little artist. I showed her the new moves toward night. She's essentially as elegant as a willow wand."
All things considered, a man with a limp couldn't move. Or then again could he?
A Thomas Jefferson signature went subsequently to pay for twenty moving illustrations. Could the incomparable Democrat turn in his grave? However what were ink scratches made by a dead hand as against every one of the implications of affection and life?
Evans purchased a phonograph, and new records. He rehearsed at the entire hours, to the extraordinary enlightenment of old Mary, who washed dishes and cleaned floors in timed euphorias.
He took Baldy and Edith to tea at the enormous lodgings, and hit the dance floor with Edith. He was sorry, however kept at it. "I'm clumsy."
Edith was thoughtful and intrigued. She welcomed the two young men to her home, where there was a music

room with a supernatural floor. Once in a while the three were separated from everyone else, and some of the time Towne came in and moved as well, and Adelaide Laramore and Eloise Harper.

Towne moved very well. Regardless of his avoirdupois he was light on his feet. He practiced continually. That's what he felt assuming he lost his midsection line all would be finished. He proved unable, in any case, to consistently control his craving. Thus the sugar in his tea, and different extravagances.

Baldy kept in touch with Jane of their evening frivols.

"You ought to see us! Eloise Harper hitting the dance floor with Evans, and old Towne and his Adelaide! What's more, Edith and I! We're a beautiful pair, on the off chance that I truly do say it. We miss you, and consistently wish you were with us. Some of the time it appears to be practically coldblooded to do things that you can't share. Be that as it may, it's doing a great deal for Evans. Strange thing, the unfortunate old chap goes, maybe his life relied on it.

"We are welcome to feast with the Townes on Christmas Eve. Some class, what? By we, I mean myself and the Follettes. Edith and Mrs. Follette see a ton of one another, and Mrs. Follette is delighted! You know how she cherishes something like that — Society with a major S.

"There will be only our group and Mrs. Laramore for supper, and after that a major outfit ball.

"I will go as a page in red. What's more, Evans will be a priest and sing Christmas tunes. Edith Towne is wild about his voice. He took a seat at the piano one day in the music room, and she heard him. Jane, his voice is great — it forever was, you know, however we haven't heard it of late. Unfortunate old chap — he is by all accounts getting. Edith says it makes her need to cry to see him, however she's assisting all she with canning.

"Gracious, she's a dear and a sweetheart, Janey. Also, I don't have the foggiest idea what I will do about it. I don't bring anything to the table for her. Be that as it may, essentially I can revere ... I shan't look past that....

"Also, presently, minimal old things, deal with yourself, and don't believe we're messing about and failing to remember you, for we're not. Indeed, even Merrymaid and the pack feline look thoughtful when your name is referenced. They share the library hearth with Rusty. The old individual is on his feet now, not much the more regrettable for his mishap.

"Love to Judy and Bob, and the youngsters. Furthermore, a kiss or two for my own Janey."

Jane, having perused the letter, laid it down with a feeling of unadulterated sadness. Evans and Eloise Harper! Towne and his Adelaide! A Christmas ensemble ball! Evans singing for Edith Towne!

Evans' own letters told her little. They were beloved letters, giving her fresh insight about Sherwood, loaded with thoughtfulness and compassion, full for sure of a specific profound strength

— that helped her in the weighty days. In any case, he had portrayed delicately his own exercises. — He had maybe wondered whether or not to tell her that he could be cheerful without her.

In any case, Evans was upset. He did the things he had delineated for himself, however he was unable to do them happily as the Boy had done. For how is it that he could be happy with Jane away? He had snapshots of depression so extreme that they nearly lowered him. He came upon one passage in his journal with enthusiasm.

"Had a day with the Boy Scouts. Climbed up through Montgomery County. Gotten a few little shiners in the rivulet and cooked them. Grapes thick in the Glen. The young men resembled little Bacchuses, and hung themselves in foods grown from the ground. They are fine colleagues. I have no tolerance with individuals who view young men as only little creatures. Why their fantasies! What's more, they are timid about them! Occasionally they hold nothing back from me — and I can see the fineness that is under the external outside layer. They lie under the trees with me, and we talk as we follow the street."

Young men — — ! That was all there was to it! He'd reach out to them once more. Furthermore, he did. There were two, Sandy Stoddard and Arthur Lane, who came over and sat by the library fire with Rusty and the two felines, and popped corn, and needed to catch wind of the conflict.

From the beginning when they discussed it, Evans wouldn't talk — yet a second showed up when he found flaring words to show them how he had an outlook on it.

"I know a ton of colleagues," said Sandy Stoddard, "who say that America could never have gone into it in the event that she'd known a great deal of things. Also, that the greater part of the ones who returned feel that they were simply — tricked — — "

"Assuming they feel as such, they are fools themselves," said Evans, not long from now.

"Indeed, they're all tossing blocks at us presently," said Sandy. "France and Great Britain, and most of them. At the point when you read the papers you feel as though America was punk — — "

"Sandy," said Evans, gradually, going after the right words since this kid should know reality — "America is rarely punk. We're human, similar to the remainder of the world. We're egotistical like every other person. In any case, we're thoughtful. Furthermore, the vast majority of us actually have confidence in God. I've gone through a ton," he was flushed with the feeling of the closeness of his admission; "you young men can't at any point understand what I've gone through except if you go through it some time or another yourselves. In any case, consistently I say thanks to God kneeling down that I was a piece of a campaign that accepted it was battling for the right. We who went in with that thought emerged from it with that thought. That is all I can say regarding it — and I'd rehash it."

As he remained there on the hearth-floor covering, the young men looked at him with amazement in their eyes. They knew devoted enthusiasm when they saw it, and here in this wrecked man was a pride which appeared to make him a pinnacle above them. They felt for the second as though his head contacted the stars.

"Try not to misconstrue me," Evans proceeded; "war is damnation. Also, the majority of us tracked down revulsions more awful than any terrifying dream. In any case, we learned a certain thing, that passing isn't terrible. It is caring and helpful. What's more, there's something past."

"Well," said Sandy Stoddard, "I'm happy you said that."

Yet, Arthur Lane didn't talk. He saw Evans through a murkiness of legendary love. He saw him, as well, with a radiance of suffering. The glass of the photo on the shelf had been patched. There was the youthful trooper, attractive and fearless in his uniform. Also, here was his apparition — return to say that it was all — worth while....

Relationships with these young men cleared up numerous things for Evans. They had standards which should not be broken. Not to their young excitement should be brought the cynicism of a scattered brain — and tormented soul. They should have reality. Furthermore, the reality of the situation was this. That men who had set out their lives to save others had seen an unforgettable vision. He thought about the number of his companions, even now, in the criticism of after-war misleading publicity would forfeit the memory of that high moment....

Other than the young men, Evans had another companion. He played an unconventional game with the scarecrow. He went frequently and hung over the wall that hermit the frozen field. He chased up new garments and balanced them on the shaking figure — a jacket and a delicate cap. It appeared to be something magnanimous to dress him with warmth. Sooner or later somebody took the jacket, and Evans found the unfortunate thing stripped. It provided him with a feeling of shock to find two crossed sticks wherever there had been the similarity to a man. However, once more, he attempted. This time with an old shower robe and an offensive cap. "It will keep you warm until spring, old chap...."

The scarecrow and his style changes turned into an issue of much conversation among the negroes. Since Evans' visits were nighttime, the situation had an impact of secrecy until the wraparound broadcast its proprietor. "Fog' Evans done with' day e'ry day," old Mary told Mrs. Follette. "Whuffor he spruce up the day old scarecrow in de fiel'?"

"What scarecrow?"

Old Mary made sense of, and that evening Mrs. Follette told her child, "The darkies are getting strange notions. Did you truly make it happen?"

His grave eyes were lit briefly. "It's simply an impulse of mine, Mumsie. I had a kind of individual inclination — — "

"How strange!"

"Not quite so strange as you would suspect." He returned to his book. Nobody however Jane ought to know reality.

Thus he played the game. Working in his office, hitting the dance floor with Edith and Baldy, chumming with the young men, sprucing up the scarecrow. It appeared to be once in a while a frantic game — there were hours in which he grappled with questions. At any point might he at some point get back? Could he? There were times when it appeared he proved unable. There were evenings when he didn't rest. Hours that he spent on his knees....

So the December days sped, and it was only seven days before Christmas that Evans read the accompanying in his little book. "Feasted with the Prestons. Recounted father's ham story. — Great hit. Potomac frozen solid. Skated in the evening glow with Florence Preston. — Great trick — home to hot cocoa."

Yet again the Potomac was frozen solid. Florence Preston was hitched. However, he mustn't allow what to pass. The young man Evans would have shivered with the prospect of that frozen stream.

It was after supper, and Evans was in his room. He chased up Baldy. "Look here, old chap, there's skating on the stream. Mightn't we at any point take Sandy and Arthur with us and have a little while of it? Your vehicle will get the job done."

Baldy set out his book. "I have no philanthropies on a night like this. Moonlight. I'll take you and the young men and afterward I'll proceed to get Edith Towne." He was on his feet. "I'll hit her up now — — "

The little kids were upbeat and wild over the arrangement. At the point when they arrived at the ice, and Evans' faltering leg took steps to be a block, the young people took him among them, and away they cruised in the supernatural world — three musketeers of good cooperation and tomfoolery.

Baldy, having brought Edith, put on her skates, and they took off like birds. She was all in warm white fleece — with white furs, and Baldy wore a white sweater and cap. The silver of the night appeared to dress them in sparkling reinforcement.

Baldy expressed things to her that made her heartbeats thump. She ended up somewhat terrified.

"You're a particularly sweet-hearted writer. In any case, life isn't at all what you think it is."

"What do I suppose?"

"Gracious, all mountains and pinnacles and evening glow evenings."

"Indeed, it tends to be — — "

"Dear kid, it can't. I have no deceptions."

"You assume you haven't."

It was late when finally they removed their skates and Edith welcomed them all to return home with her. "We'll have something hot. I'm basically as eager as twelve bears."

The young men snickered. "So am I," said Sandy Stoddard. However, Arthur didn't say anything. His eyes were involved in the prohibition of his tongue. Edith shifted focus over to him like some holy messenger directly from paradise. He had never seen anybody so wonderful.

Thus, pressed in Baldy's Ford, they made the excursion. The two little children had an Arabian Nights' inclination as they were driven through the extraordinary lobby with its overhangs, thus to the immense kitchen.

The workers had hit the hay, all aside from Waldron — who drove the way, and offered his administrations.

"No, we'll do it without anyone's help, Waldron," Miss Towne told him. "Is Uncle Fred ready?"

"No, Miss Towne."

"Indeed, assuming he comes, let him know where we are."

"Excellent, Miss Towne," Waldron pulled out amazingly, according to the young men upon him.

Edith provided them with the opportunity of the astonishing cooler, which was white as milk and as large as a house, and they delivered with some delay viands which appeared to be pretty much as unbelievable as the remainder of it — cold dish chickens with white ornaments on their legs, a plate of salad with designs on top of it in red peppers and minimal green buttons which Evans said were tricks — the remaining parts of a celebrated kind of Charlotte Russe — a fortified undertaking with sugar coated organic products.

"Do they eat things like this consistently?" Sandy asked Evans, with something like wonderment, "or am I dreamin'?"

Evans gestured. "Some banquet, isn't it, old chap?" He was warmed by the brilliance of the freckled innocent face. Arthur Lane, in every case less chatty, wanted to sit quiet. He was soaking himself in the environment. He had never been in a house like this. The kitchen with its framed roof, its white polish, its glimmering nickel, its firm, white painted furnishings — its white and earthy colored tiling. It was all basically as completely entrancing as the things he read about in the pixie books.

"Presently the kitchen," he said finally to Towne, "what's it so enormous for? Ain't there just three of them in the family?"

"Indeed."

"Indeed, there are six of us at home, and you could place four of our kitchens into this. Also, that cooler — it's so huge you could live in it. You know, Mr. Follette, it's greater than our scout tents."

"Indeed, it is," Evans grinned at him. "Indeed, when individuals have such a lot of cash, they assume they need things."

"I'd like it." The kid was anxious. "Couldn't you?"

"I don't know."

"Hmm — all things considered, I am — — " and youthful Arthur headed toward work it out with Sandy.

Evans, left to himself, pondered. Did he need cash? An extraordinary fortune? With Jane? The colossal quiet house with every one of its workers? Jane, herself, following up the steps in every one of the amazing curtains forced upon her by elegant modistes? Jane, miles from him toward the finish of that enormous table in the extraordinary lounge area? Were these his fantasies? For Jane? He realized they were not. At the point when he thought about her, he thought about a little house. Of a lounge room where a fire shines brilliantly whose windows view a little nursery — crocuses and hyacinths in the spring, roses in June, snow in winter, with every one of the birds coming up for Jane to take care of them. A library with books to the roof, and himself perusing Jane. A kitchen, a sparkling spot, with a fresh house cleaner to save Jane from drudgery. Two fresh house cleaners, maybe, sometime in the future, assuming there were youngsters.
He asked something like that. Why, it was all the world for a man....

## Part XVI

## THE COSTUME BALL

So Christmas Eve came, and the ensemble ball at the Townes'. There were, as Baldy had told Jane, only six of them at supper. Cousin Annabel was still in bed, and it was Adelaide Laramore who made the 6th. Edith had told Mrs. Follette honestly that she wished Adelaide had not been inquired.

"Yet, she looked for it. She generally does. She compliments Uncle Fred and he gets bulldozed."

Baldy brought Evans and Mrs. Follette in his little Ford. They tracked down Mrs. Laramore and Frederick, currently in the drawing-room. Edith had not descended.

"She is in every case late," Frederick griped, "and she won't ever apologize."

Baldy, luxurious and thin, in his page's red, remained in the lobby and watched Edith slip the steps. She appeared to rise up out of the shadows of the upper gallery like a shaft of light. She was all in shiny green, her nearby gripping robe supported with pearls, her hair grouped with mistletoe.

He met her midway. "You shouldn't have worn it," he said immediately.

"The mistletoe? No difference either way."

"You will entice all men to kiss you."

"Men should oppose enticement."

"Indeed, sovereigns order," he grinned at her, "and sovereigns ask — — "

She was dubious of his importance.

"How about I at any point request kisses?"

"You may. Sometime in the future."

Her blue eyes consumed. "I figure you don't exactly have the foggiest idea what you are talking about."

"I do, dear woman. Be that as it may, we won't fight about it."

She changed to less risky subjects.

"I'm late for supper. Is Uncle Fred thundering?"

"Pretty much. Furthermore, Mrs. Laramore is murmuring."

They rather underhandedly partook in their giggle to the detriment of a more established age, and went in together to track down Frederick frigid with resentment.

Waldron reported supper, and Frederick with Mrs. Follette on his arm went before the others. Baldy and Edith came last.

"What number of moves would you say you will give me?"

"Not quite as many as I'd like. Being a lady, I will need to split myself between many."

"Cut yourself up into little stars in a manner of speaking. All things considered, you understand what Browning says of a star? 'Mine has opened its spirit to me — consequently I love it'!"

His tone was light, however her heart thought twice. There was something about this kid so completely captivating. He had set her on a platform, and he revered her. At the point when she said that she was not worth adoring, he told her, "You don't have the foggiest idea — — "

She was abnormally quiet during supper. With Evans on one side of her and Baldy on the other she had little need to strive. Baldy was generally sufficient to any conversational duty, and Evans, regardless of his priest's propensity, was not somber. He was, fairly, similar to some alluring youthful minister who stepped back for the second time in the world.

He showed himself a cheerful storyteller — and covered every one of Frederick's with one of his own. His mom was pleased with him. She felt

that life was taking on new viewpoints — this kinship with the Townes — her child's rising strength and social simplicity — the ribbon outfit which she wore and which had been purchased with a Dickens' handout. What more might she at some point inquire? She was quiet and fulfilled.
Adelaide, on the opposite side of Frederick Towne, was not quiet and fulfilled. She was looking especially exquisite with a star of precious stones in her hair and sheer curtains of rose and slightest green. "I'm anything you wish to call me," she had shared with Frederick when she came in — "an 'Night Star' or 'In the Gloaming' or 'Luminosity.' Perhaps 'A Rose of Yesterday' — — " she had put it rather thoughtfully.
He had been chivalrous yet deadened. "You are too youthful to even think about discussing previous days," he had said, yet his look had held not the smallest smidgen of chivalry. She felt that she had, maybe, been imprudent to help him to remember her age.
She was even more upset, when, towards the finish of supper, he rose and gave an impromptu speech. "To little Jane Barnes, A Merry Christmas."
They generally stood up. There was a subsequent quiet. Evans drank as though he participated in a holy observance.
Then Edith said, "It appears to be practically merciless to be content, doesn't it, when things are so difficult for her?"
Adelaide mediated superfluously, "I ought to hate to spend Christmas in Chicago."

There was no reaction, so she went to Frederick. "Couldn't Miss Barnes leave her sister for a couple of days?"
"No," he told her, "she proved unable."
She endured, "I'm certain you didn't believe she should miss the ball."
"I gave my all to get her here. Conversed with her at a significant distance, however she was unable to see it."
"You are so great hearted, Ricky."
Frederick could be savage at minutes, and her determination was bothersome. "Goodness, look here, Adelaide, it wasn't altogether for her. I need her here myself."
She sat unmoving, her eyes on her plate. At the point when she talked again it was of different things. "Did you hear that Delafield is returning?"
"Who told you?"
"Eloise Harper. Benny's sister saw Del at Miami. She is certain he is hoping to wed the other young lady."
"Awful taste, I call it."
"Everyone is insane to know what her identity is."
"Have they any thought?"
"No. Benny's sister said he discussed getting hitched. Be that as it may, he wouldn't agree to the slightest peep about the lady."
"I scarcely figure he will find Edith heart-broken." Towne looked across the table. Edith was not wearing the willow. No shadow damaged her wonderful face. Her eyes were clear and sparkling pools of sweet happiness.
Her uncle was pleased with that high-held head. He and Edith could not

generally get along. In any case, by Jove, he was pleased with her.
"No, she's not heart-broken," Adelaide's cool tone upset his appearance, "she is getting her heart retouched."
"Your meaning could be a little clearer."
"They are an alluring pair, little Jane and her sibling. What's more, the kid has lost his head."
"Over Edith? Goodness, indeed, she messes with him; there's nothing serious in it."
"Try not to be excessively certain. She's intrigued."
"What compels you to demand that?" peevishly.
"I know the signs, dear man," the feline appeared to murmur, yet she had hooks.
What's more, it was Adelaide who was on the right track. Edith had come to the information that evening of how Badly affected her.
As she entered the dance hall men swarmed around her. "Why," they asked, "do you wear mistletoe, if you would rather not pay the relinquish?"
Upheld against one of the marble support points, she held them off. "I would like to pay it, yet not to any of you."
Her straightforwardness redirected them. "Who is the fortunate man?"
"He is here. In any case, he doesn't realize he is fortunate."
They thought she was kidding. Be that as it may, she was not. What's more, on the opposite side of the marble support point a page in red turned in,

with happiness and dread in his heart.
"How quick we are going. How quick."
It was moving until late, then, at that point, the drapes toward the finish of the room were stepped back, and the tree was uncovered. It transcended to the roof, a sparkling, lovely thing. It was weighted with gifts for everyone, fabulous toys, the vast majority of them, costly, pointless.
Evans, remaining back of the group, knew about the vacancy, all things considered, Gracious, what had there been all through the night to make men consider the Babe who had been brought into the world at Bethlehem? The gifts of the Wise Men? Maybe. Gold and frankincense and myrrh? One should not judge too barely. Keeping simplicity in these extravagant days was hard.
However he was miserable, and when Eloise Harper energized him, dressed fairly meagerly as a dryad, and gave him a silly monkey on a stick, she appeared to propose a pagan saturnalia instead of anything Christian and edified.
"A monkey for a priest," said Eloise. "Mr. Follette, your cassock is appalling. Be that as it may, you realize you are a whited tomb."
"Am I?"
"Obviously. I'll wager you will never say your requests."
She moved away, oblivious that her words had penetrated him. What reason had she to imagine that any of this implied more to him than it did to her? Had he borne an observer to the confidence that was inside him?

What's more, was it inside him?
What's more, if not, why?
He remained there with his silly monkey on his stick, while around him whirled a snickering, yelling swarm. Why, the thing was a festival, not a consecrated festival. Was it basically impossible that he could tolerate witnessing?
Edith had requested that he sing the old numbers, "Woman, get up and prepare your pies," and "I saw three ships cruising." Evans couldn't care less about the lady who cheated her pies on Christmas day toward the beginning of the day, or the lovely young ladies who whistled and sang — on Christmas day in the first part of the day.
At the point when every one of the gifts had been dispersed the lights in the room were ended up. The main light was the brilliant luster which enclosed the tree.
In his priest's robe, inside that circle of light, Evans appeared to be a magical figure. He appeared, as well, fittingly austere, with his silver hair, the exhausted lines of his old-youthful face.
Yet, his voice was new and unmistakable. Furthermore, the melody he sang quieted the extraordinary room into quiet.
"O little town of Bethlehem,
How still we see you lie,
Above thy profound and dreamless rest,
The quiet stars go by;
However in thy dull roads shineth,
The never-ending light,

The expectations and fears of the relative multitude of years
I will meet with you to-night."
He sang as though he were separated from everyone else in some tremendous curved space, underneath towers that came towards Heaven, behind some grille that isolated him from the world.
"For Christ is brought into the world of Mary,
Also, assembled all above,
While humans rest, the holy messengers keep
Their watch of pondering affection.
O, morning stars together
Broadcast the heavenly birth!
What's more, acclaims sing to God the King
Furthermore, harmony to men on the planet."
Furthermore, presently he couldn't help suspecting that he sang not to that horde of improved faces, not to those people in sparkling silks and silks, not to Jane who was far away, but rather to those other people who squeezed close — his friends across the Great Divide!
So he had sung to them in the medical clinic, sitting up in his limited bed — and the majority of the ones who had listened were — gone.
"O, sacred offspring of Bethlehem,
Drop to us, we ask,
Project out our wrongdoing and enter in,
Be brought into the world in us to-day.
We hear the Christmas holy messengers
The incredible happy news tell:
'Gracious come to us, stay with us,

Our Lord Emmanuel.'"
As the final words rang out his crowd appeared to wake with a murmur. Then the lights went up. However, the priest had evaporated!
Evans left word with Baldy that he would return home on the streetcar. "I'm not exactly up to the dinner what not. Will you take care of Mother?"
"Obviously. Say, Evans, that melody was first class. Edith believes that you should sing another."
"Will you tell her I can't? Please accept my apologies. In any case, the last time I sang that was for my colleagues — in France. Furthermore, it — got me — — "
"It got me, as well," Baldy trusted; "made this appear — senseless."
So Evans abandoned him all the young and giggling and happiness, and took the last streetcar out to Castle Manor. He had a long stroll after the ride, yet the virus air was invigorating, the sky was brimming with stars and the night was exceptionally still. Gracious, that being out in that still and star-lit night was so great!
At the point when he arrived at Castle Manor he passed the stable en route to the house. He opened the entryway and searched in. There was a lamp, faintly lit, and he could see the cows laying on their beds of straw — extraordinary faint animals, possessing a scent like milk and feed — quite looked at, enigmatic.
He entered and plunked down. He felt alleviated and supported by the serenity of the moronic monsters — the persuasive quiet.

He was happy he had gotten away from the commotion of the ensemble ball — from Eloise and her sort. However the Man brought into the world at Bethlehem had not gotten away. He had gone among the hoards — talking.

Well ... it couldn't be anticipated, could it, that men in these days would agree to a young lady like Eloise Harper, "For unto you is conceived this day in the city of David, a Savior which is Christ the Lord"?

Individuals didn't express such things amongst people who value proper etiquette ... also, in the event that they didn't, same difference either way. What's more, in the event that they did, could the world tune in?

## Part XVII

## NEWS FOR THE TOWN-CRIER

It was not long before New Year's that Lucy Logan carried a letter for Frederick Towne to sign, and when he had completed she said, "Mr. Towne, I'm unfortunately I won't work any longer. So if you don't mind, kindly acknowledge my renunciation?"

He showed his shock. "What's wrong? Might it be said that we are adequate for you?"

"It isn't so much that." She went back and forth on, "I will be hitched, Mr. Towne."

"Hitched?" He was without a moment's delay celebratory. "That is something charming for you, and I mustn't ruin it by letting you know how hard it will be to track down somebody to have your spot."

"I suppose that you will have Miss Dale? She's actually quite great."

Frederick was interested. What sort of darling had won this tranquil Lucy? Most likely some assistant or sales rep. "And the man? Decent individual, I trust — — "

"Extremely decent, Mr. Towne," she flushed, and her way appeared to disallow further addressing. She disappeared, and he provided requests to the clerk to see that she had an expansion in how much her last check was. "She will require a few pretty things. What's more, when we become familiar with the date we can give her a present."

So on Saturday night Lucy left, and on the next Monday a card was raised to Edith Towne.

She read it. "Lucy Logan? I don't really accept that I know her," she told the house cleaner.

"She says she is from Mr. Towne's office, and that it is significant."

Presently Josephine, the parlor servant, had a decent feeling of the decencies which she had gained from Waldron, who was not on the job in that frame of mind of the house in the first part of the day. So she had given Lucy a seat in the extraordinary lobby. Waldron had underlined that business guests and social inferiors should never be guided into the drawing-room. The grade beneath Lucy's was, without a doubt, sent around to a side entryway.

Nonetheless, there Lucy sat — in a dull blue cape and a little blue cap, and she rose as Edith came dependent upon her.

"Gracious, how about we go where we can be agreeable," Edith said, and

drove the way through the dim and white drawing-room past the peacock screen, to the shining warmth of the fire.
They were an incredible differentiation, these two ladies. Edith in a tea-outfit of light yellow was the final say regarding stylishness. Lucy, in her unobtrusive blue, had no cases to qualify.
However, Lucy was not anxious. "Miss Towne," she said, "I have left your uncle's office. Did he tell you?"
"No. Uncle Fred seldom talks about business."
With trademark straightforwardness Lucy came immediately direct. "I have something I should talk about with you. I don't know whether I am doing the savvy thing. However, it is the main legit thing."
"I can't envision what you need to say."
"No you can't. It's this — — " she wavered, then, at that point, talked with a worker. "I'm the young lady Mr. Simms is infatuated with. He needs to return and wed me."
Edith's fingers got at the arm of the seat. "Do you imply that it was a result of you — that he didn't wed me?"
"Indeed. He used to come to the workplace when he was in Washington and direct letters. Also, we impeded conversing with one another. He appeared to appreciate it, and he wasn't similar to certain men — who are simply — senseless. Furthermore, I started to contemplate him a great deal. However, I didn't allow him to see it. What's more, — he told me a short time later, he was

continuously considering me. Also, the morning of your big day he boiled down to the workplace — to bid farewell.' 'He said he — just needed to. What's more, — indeed, he let it out that he cherished me, and didn't have any desire to wed you. However, he said he would need it to happen with it. Also, — and I let him know he should not, Miss Towne."

Edith gazed at her. "Do you imply that what he did was your issue?"

"Indeed," Lucy's face was white, "to put it that way. I let him know he hadn't any option to wed you in the event that he cherished me." She delayed, lifted her eyes to Edith's with a look of allure. "Miss Towne, I keep thinking about whether you are adequately large to accept that it was on the grounds that I minded so much — and not due to his cash?"

It was a test. Edith had been prepared to spill out her rage on the top of this young lady to whom she owed the embarrassment of the previous weeks, however there was about Lucy a specific solidness, a fortitude which was capturing.

"You assume you love him?" she requested.

"I realize I do. What's more, you don't. You won't ever have. What's more, he didn't cherish you. Why — assuming that he ought to lose each penny to-morrow, and I needed to jaunt down the street with him, I'd do it happily. Also, you wouldn't. You couldn't need him except if he could give you all that you have now, OK? Could you, Miss Towne?"

Edith's feeling of equity directed her response. "No," she wound up suddenly conceding. "Assuming I needed to jaunt the streets with him, I'd be worn out."

"I think he knew that, Miss Towne. He let me know that in the event that he didn't wed you, your heart wouldn't be broken. That it would just damage your pride."

Edith had a snapshot of insane jollity. How they had talked her over. Her sweetheart — and her uncle's transcriber! What a misfortune it had been! Furthermore, what a satire!

She inclined forward a bit, locking her fingers about her knees. "I wish you'd fill me in regarding it."

"I don't know exactly what to say. Then again, actually we've been keeping in touch with one another. I said that we should wait for 90 days. It didn't appear reasonable for you to have him wed too early."

Uncle Fred's transcriber sorry for her!

"Go on," Edith said, rigidly.

So Lucy recounted the basic story. What's more, in telling it showed herself so credulous, so resolute, that Edith knew about a rising admiration for the one who had her spot in the core of her sweetheart. She saw that Lucy had arrived at this meeting with no soul of victory. She had feared it, however had felt it her obligation. "I figured it would be simpler for you assuming that you knew it before others did."

Edith's temple was weaved in a slight glare. "The situation has been generally horrendous," she said. "When are you going to wed him?"

"I told him on St. Valentine's day. It appeared — heartfelt."

Sentiment and Del! Edith had an unexpected light. Why, this was the very thing that he had needed, and she had given him none of it! She had snickered at him — been his great confidant. Little Lucy loved him — and had set St. Valentine's day for the wedding!

There was nothing little about Edith Towne. She knew fineness when she saw it, and she had a sensation of modesty within the sight of little Lucy.

"I think it was my shortcoming as much as Del's," she expressed. "I ought to never have said 'OK.' People haven't any option to wed who feel as we did."

"Goodness," Lucy said euphorically, "how dear of you to say that. Miss Towne, I generally realized you were — enormous. Be that as it may, I didn't dream you were so lovely." Tears wet her cheeks. "You're simply — grand," she said, cleaning them away.

"No, I'm not." Edith's eyes were on the fire. "Regularly, I am somewhat glad and — scornful. In the event that you had come seven days prior — — " Her voice fell away into quiet as she actually gazed at the fire.

Lucy took a gander at her inquisitively. "Seven days prior?"

Edith gestured. "Do you like fantasies? Indeed, when there was a princess. What's more, a page came and sang — under her window." The fire murmured and snapped. "What's more, the princess — preferred the melody — — "

"Gracious," said Lucy, faintly.

"All things considered, that is all," said Edith; "I don't have a clue about the end." She extended herself sluggishly. Her free sleeves, drifting away from her uncovered arms, gave the impact of wings. Lucy, seeing her, considered how it had at any point happened that Delafield might have diverted his eyes from that interesting excellence to her own unexceptional beauty.

She stood up. "I can't tell you how appreciative I am that I came."

"You won't take off yet," Edith told her. "I believe that you should eat with me. Higher up. You should let me know every one of your arrangements."

"I don't have quite a large number. What's more, I truly oughtn't to remain."

"No difference either way. I need you. Kindly don't say no."

So up they went, with the irritated parlor house cleaner talking through the cylinder to the storeroom. "Miss Towne needs a lunch meeting for two, Mr. Waldron. In her room. According to something decent, she, and a lot of it."

Little Lucy had never seen such a room as the one to which Edith drove her. The entire house was, to be sure, a fantasy royal residence. However it was the environment with which her darling would before long encompass her. She had an inclination nearly of frenzy. How might she manage a servant like Alice, who was assisting Josephine with setting up the collapsing table, spreading the blanketed material, and getting the hot silver dishes?

As though Edith divined her idea, she said when the house cleaners had left, "Lucy, will you let me exhort?"
"Obviously, Miss Towne."
"Try not to attempt to be — like most of us. Like Del's own group, I mean. He fell head over heels for you since you were unique. He will believe you should remain — unique."
"In any case, I will have such a long way to go."
Edith was eager. "What must you realize? Facades? Leave them be. Act naturally. You have nobility — and strength. It was the strength in you that won Del. You and he can have a coexistence that will mean an incredible arrangement, in the event that you will make him turn out well for you. Yet, you should not go his — — "
Lucy thought about that. "You imply that the group he is with debilitates him?"
"I mean simply that. They're complex indeed. You're what they would call — common. Goodness, be common, Lucy. Try not to be apprehensive. Be that as it may, don't take on their methodologies. You go to chapel, isn't that right? Say your requests? Trust that God's in His reality?"
Lucy's fair cheeks were flushed. "Why, obviously I do."
"Indeed, we don't — relatively few of us," said Edith. "What you must do is to show Del something. Try not to simply go cruising away with him in his yacht. Purchase a ranch over in Virginia, and assist him with making an outcome of it."
"However, he lives in New York."

"Obviously he does. Yet, he can live anywhere. He's rich to such an extent that he doesn't need to procure anything, and his office is only a fiction. You should make him work. Go in for a prevailing fashion; blooded ponies, cows, dark Berkshires. Do you have any idea what a dark Berkshire is, Lucy?"

"No, I don't."

"Indeed, it's a sort of a pig. Also, that is something ideal for yourself and Del. He truly cherishes fine stock. What's more, you and he — think about it — riding over the nation — arranging your nurseries — having a child or two." Edith was going extremely quick.

"It sounds grand," said Lucy.

"Then make it Heaven. Gracious, Lucy, Lucy, you fortunate young lady — you will wed the man you love. Live away from the world — share joy and despondency — — " She rose from the table anxiously, pushing back her seat, dropping her napkin on the floor. "Do you have at least some idea how I envy you?"

She went to the window and stood watching out. "What's more, here I sit, many days, similar to a detainee in a pinnacle — and my page sings — that was its start — and it will be the end."

"No," Lucy was intense, "you mustn't allow it to be the end. You — you should open the window, Miss Towne."

Edith returned to the table. "Open the window?" Her breath came quickly. "Open the window. Gracious, little Lucy, how wise you are...."

At the point when Lucy had gone, Alice came in and dressed Edith's hair. She found her woman insightful.
"Alice, how did they manage my wedding garments?"
It was whenever she first had referenced them. Alice, staying in fasteners, was loaded up with anxious interest.
"We put them all in the second visitor suite," she expressed; "some of them we left stuffed in the trunks similarly as they were, and some of them are held in tight racks."
"Where is the wedding dress?"
"In a storage room in a white cloth pack."
"Indeed, finish my hair and we will proceed to check it out."
Alice is trapped in the last pin. "The shroud is over a silk roller. I did it without anyone else's help, and put the cap part in a cap box."
As they entered it, the second visitor suite was weighty with the fragrance of orange blossoms. "How loathsome, Alice," Edith discharged. "For what reason didn't you discard the blossoms?"
"Miss Annabel wouldn't let me. She said you probably won't need things contacted."
"Senseless wistfulness." Edith was anxious.
The room was in all the despair of closed draperies. The dresses held tight racks, and, encased in white packs, gave a spooky impact. "They are like columns of gravestones, Alice."
"Indeed, Miss Towne," said Alice, obediently.

The housekeeper drew out the wedding dress and laid it on the bed. Edith, looking over it, was stung by the memory of the feelings which had influenced her when she had last worn it. It had appeared to deride her. She had needed to attack shreds. She had seen her own strained face in the mirror, as she had controlled herself before Alice. Then, when the housekeeper had left, she had hurled herself on the bed, and had squirmed in a distress of embarrassment.
Also, presently everything her outrage was no more. She couldn't stand Del. She couldn't stand Lucy. She even considered Uncle Fred with noble cause. What's more, the wedding outfit was, all things considered, a robe for a princess ruler. Not a robe for a princess page. A delicate grin relaxed her face.
"Alice," she said, unexpectedly, "wasn't there a little heliotrope supper dress among my linen things?"
"Indeed, Miss Towne. Casual." Alice chased in the third column of headstones until she tracked down it.
"I need long sleeves put in it. Will you tell Hardinger, and have him send a cap to coordinate?"
"Indeed, Miss Towne."
The heliotrope dress had basic and exquisite lines. It drifted in sheer magnificence from the house cleaner's hands as she held it up. "There is certainly not a prettier one in the entire part, Miss Edith."
"I like it," the scent of heliotrope drifted from stowed sachets, "and concerning the wedding outfit," Edith looked at it mindfully, "loaded it in a crate with the

cloak and other things. I believe Briggs should accept it with the note to a location that I will give him."

"Gracious, indeed, Miss Towne." Alice was highly inspired by the location. She concentrated on it when, later, she conveyed the case and the note down to Briggs.

Edith, having dispatched the crate with an enchanting note to Lucy Logan, had a sensation of elated opportunity. All the hurt and embarrassment of the wedding episode had left. She didn't mind the world's thought process of her. Her departure by Del had been material for a day's tattle — then, at that point, different things had filled the papers, had been featured and underscored. Also, why did everything matter?

The things that made a difference were those of which she had conversed with Lucy. An old house — shared interests, the remainder of it. "I would jaunt down the street with him," little Lucy had said. That was love — to count nothing hard except for its absence.

She was called to the phone, and tracked down Eloise Harper at the opposite end. "Delafield is returning," she said. "Benny has had a letter."

"Dear local proclaimer," said Edith, "you are late with your information."

"What do you mean by local proclaimer?"

"That is the very thing that we call you, dearest."

"Goodness, isn't that right?" regrettably. "All things considered, in any case, Delafield is coming back, and he will be hitched when he arrives."

"Yet, he isn't. Not until February."

"How would you be aware?"

"The lady told me."

"Who?" suspiciously.

"The lady of the hour."

Eloise wheezed. "Edith, do you have any idea about what her identity is?"

"I do indeed."

"Tell me."

"My dear, I can't. The entire world would know it."

"I swear I — — "

"Try not to swear, Eloise. You could prevaricate yourself," and Edith hung up the collector.

## Section XVIII

## AN INTERLUDE

The day after Christmas.

"Baldy, sweetheart: The activity is finished, and the specialist gives us trust. That is all that I can tell you. I haven't been permitted to see Judy, however they have allowed Bob to have a peep at her, and she grinned.

"You can envision that we have had little heart for good times. However, the infants had a delightful Christmas Day, with a tree — and stockings hung over the gas logs. How I yearned for our own little wood fire, yet the favored dears didn't have a clue about the distinction. We were unable to burn through much cash, which was lucky. The things that came from the east were so awesome. Yours, honey-kid, just you shouldn't have made the check so enormous. I shan't spend it except if it is extremely vital. Mr. Towne sent roses, heaps of them — and totally superb chocolates in a crate of gold enamel — and Edith sent a line of cut ivory dabs, and there was a blue Keats from Evans, and a ducky orange scarf from Mrs. Follette.

"I want to see the children. Julia lurched around the tree on her questionable little feet as though she were intoxicated, and afterward settled down to a cute stuffed rabbit, and Junior had a keen interest in only the red vehicle that the Townes requested for him. I appreciate Edith and her uncle. Junior is a particularly beguiling chap, with lovely habits like his father, yet with his very own will on occasion.

"I simmered a chicken for supper, and — indeed, we traversed everything. Also, presently the children are sleeping, and Bob is at the clinic, and I am keeping in touch with you. In any case, my heart is tight with dread.

"I mustn't contemplate Judy.

"Give my affection to everyone. I have had Christmas letters from Evans and Edith and Mr. Towne. Baldy, Mr. Towne needs to wed me. I haven't told you previously. It is somewhat similar to a fantasy and I won't consider it. I don't cherish him, thus, obviously, that settles it. However, he says he can make me, and, Baldy, now and again I wish that he could. It would be a particularly grand thing for the entire family. Obviously that isn't the method for taking a gander at it, yet I accept Judy needs it. She has confidence in affection in a house, however she says that affection in a royal residence may similarly fulfill, with less things to stress over.

"Some way or another that doesn't find a place with the things I've imagined. However, dreams, obviously, aren't everything....

"I needed to tell you, beloved kid. Since we've never kept things from one another. Furthermore, you've been so completely blunt about Edith. Are things a piece blue that way? Your letter seemed like it.

"Do right by yourself, old dear, and love me like never before."

Jane marked her name and stood up, extending her arms over her head. It was late and she was exceptionally worn out. An extraordinary tempest was shaking the windows. The breeze from the lake beat against the walls with the blast of firearms.

Jane pulled back the shades — there was snow with the tempest — it spun in papery shreds on the shaft of light. All sounds in the road were suppressed. She had a feeling of suffocation — as though the tempest squeezed upon her — closing her in. She went into the following room and checked the children out. Gracious, how might they respond assuming anything happened to Judy? How might Bob respond? She tried not to look forward.

She strolled the floor, a strained little figure, battling against dread. The tempest had turned into a whistling disorder. She gave a cry of help when the entryway opened and her brother by marriage entered.

"I'm half-frozen, Janey. It was a battle to traverse. The vehicles are halted on every one of the surface lines."

"How is Judy?"

"Standing her ground. What's more, coincidentally, Janey, that companion

of yours, Towne, sent one more bundle of roses. Fine, I call it. She's not satisfied."
"It's pleasant of him."
"Hmm, I wish I had his cash."
"Cash isn't all that matters, Bobby."
"It implies a ton during such a critical point in time." His face wore a stressed glare. Jane realized that Judy's clinic costs were shocking, and charges were stacking up.
"I work like a nigger," Bob said, sadly, "and we've never been in the red."
"At the point when Judy is well, things will appear to be more splendid, Bob." She laid her hand on his arm.
He gazed toward her and there was dread in his eyes. "Jane, she should recover. I can't confront losing her."
"We mustn't consider that. What's more, I'm presently in the kitchen and I'll make you some espresso." Jane was consistently common sense. That's what she knew, warmed and took care of, he would see things in an unexpected way.
However despite her way of thinking, Jane lay conscious for quite a while that evening. What's more, later her fantasies were of Judy — of Judy, and a dim and loathsome ghost which pursued....
The following day she went to the clinic and took Junior with her.
When he saw his mom in bed, Junior inquired, "Do you like it, Mother-dear?"
"Like what, dear?"
"Resting in the daytime?"
"I don't necessarily rest." She checked Jane out. "Does little Julia miss me? I contemplate her in the evening."

Jane understood what Judy's heart needed. "She misses you. I know it when she gets some distance from me. Maybe I oughtn't to tell you. However, I thought you'd prefer to know."

"I would like to be aware," said Judy, hotly. "I don't believe that they should neglect. Jane, you mustn't at any point let them — neglect."

Jane felt as though she had been struck by a staggering blow. She was, briefly, amidst a mixed up universe, wherein only one thing was clear. Judy wasn't certain of recovering!

Judy, with her earthy colored eyes contemplative, went on: "Junior, do you need Mother back in your own pleasant house?"

"Will you make treats?"

"Indeed, sweetheart."

"Then, at that point, I need you back. Auntie Janey made treats, and she had hardly any familiarity with the raisins."

"Mother knows how to treat men with raisin eyes. Moms know a great deal of things that ants don't, sweetheart."

"All things considered, I wish you'd return." He remained by the side of the bed. "I might want to lay down with you to-night. May I, Mother-dear?"

"Not to-night, sweetheart. However, you may when I return home."

Yet, days passed and weeks, and Judy didn't get back home. Also, the first of February found her still in that restricted emergency clinic bed. Also, it was in February that Frederick Towne composed that he was coming to Chicago. "I will have just a day, however I should see you."

Jane didn't know that she believed him should come. He had been generally excellent to them all, and he had not, in his letter, squeezed for a response unduly. Be that as it may, she knew whether he came, he would inquire. The following time she went to the clinic, she told Judy of his normal appearance. "To-morrow."
"Goodness, Jane, how brilliant."
"Is it? I don't know, Judy."
"It would be awesome assuming you'd acknowledge him, Jane."
"Be that as it may, I'm not in adoration with him."
Judy, somewhat somber, with her dark plaits on each side of her white face, said, "Janey, do you have any idea that not one young lady in 1,000 gets an opportunity to wed a man like Frederick Towne?"
There was a winded energy about the invalid which cautioned Jane.
"Presently, dear, what genuine distinction will it make in the event that I don't wed him? There are different men on the planet."
"Sway and I were discussing it," Judy's voice was agonizingly enthusiastic, "of how awesome it would be for — we all."
For us all. Judy and Bob and the infants! It was whenever Jane first had considered her marriage with Towne an exit plan for Judy and Bob....
From his lodging right now of appearance, Towne hit Jane up.
"Could it be said that you are happy I'm here?"
"Obviously."
"Try not to say it that way."
"How might I say it?"

"As though you would not joke about this. Do you have at least some idea how bone chilling little you are? Your letters resembled glazed cakes."
She chuckled. "They were everything I could manage."
"I don't trust it. In any case, I won't discuss that at this point. When might I at any point come and see you? Furthermore, how long have you been, especially for me?"
"Not much. I can't leave the children."
"Your sister's kids. Mightn't you at any point trust the servants?"
"House cleaners? Pay attention to the man! We haven't any."
"You don't intend to let me know that you are doing the housework."
"Indeed, same difference either way. I'm solid and indeed, and the youngsters are cute."
"We will change that. I'll carry a prepared medical attendant up with me."
"Kindly don't be a despot."
"Tut, young lady," she heard his enormous chuckle via phone, "I'll carry the medical caretaker and somebody to help her, and a heap of toys to keep the youngsters calm. At the point when I need a thing, Jane, I ordinarily get it."
He and the medical attendant showed up together. A skillful house worker was to continue in a taxi. Jane dissented. "It appears to be horribly overbearing."
They were separated from everyone else in the front room. Miss Martin had, on the double, stolen the youngsters away to unload the toys.

Frederick snickered. "All things considered, what are you going to do about it? You can't put me out."
"Yet, I can decline to go with you" — there was the fresh note in her voice which generally confused him.
"However, you will not do that, Jane." He held out his hand to her, drew her a little towards him.
She delivered herself, flushing. "I'm not exactly certain what I should do."
"Why consider 'oughts'? We will simply play a piece together, Jane. There's nothing more to it. What's more, you're a particularly worn out young lady, right?"
His compassion was consoling. Everyone rested on Jane. It was magnificent to move her weights to this resilient man who provided his orders like a ruler.
"Indeed, I am worn out. Furthermore, assuming the children will be OK — — "

"Great. Presently run in and see Miss Martin, and I think you'll be fulfilled."
Jane tracked down Junior blissfully over Noah's Ark, with every one of the creatures dressed in fur and hair, and the birds in quills, and little Julia nestled against the medical caretaker's white bosom, excited with interest over the Three Kittens.
"They'll be good, Miss Barnes," Miss Martin said, grinning.
Jane murmured with alleviation. "It will appear great just a little."
"You perceive how I get everything I could possibly want," Frederick said, as he helped her into the enormous, employed limousine. "I generally get it."

"It is somewhat grand right now," Jane conceded, "yet you shouldn't even need to believe that it lays out a point of reference."

"Couldn't it be consistently — superb?"

"I don't know. You have the makings of a — Turk."

However she giggled as she said it, and he snickered, as well. He was actually quite attractive, bronzed and splendid and huge — and with that quality of gay yielding. She jumped at the chance to sit alongside him, and pay attention to the things he needed to tell her. It was quiet after every one of the arduous days.

That's what she knew whether she wedded Towne life would be consistently this way. A celebrated presence. She would be like Curlylocks of the nursery rhyme....

"What are you grinning at?" Frederick requested. His eyes as they met hers consumed a little. Jane was half-covered in a dark fur robe — with just the white oval of her face and her little dim cap appearing above it.

"Nursery rhymes." The grin developed.

"Which one?"

"Curlylocks."

"I don't recall it. Gracious, indeed, by Jove, I do. She was the lady who sat on a pad and sewed a fine crease, and devoured strawberries, sugar and cream?"

"Indeed."

"Great. That is how I need to help you. You know it?"

"Indeed. Yet, it very well may be — dreary."

"What better thing could happen to you than to have somebody deal with you?"
Jane sat up. "Goodness, I need to live," she expressed, nearly with wildness. "I'd prefer not to think my better half was only a kind of — feather pad."
"Is that the manner in which you think about me?" His vanity was immaculate. She didn't, obviously, would not joke about this.
"No. However, love is life. I would rather not miss it."
"You won't miss it assuming that you wed me. I swear it, Jane, I'll make you love me."
He was dead sincere. Furthermore, regardless of herself she was influenced by his demeanor of conviction.
"Goodness, we mustn't discuss it," she said, a piece energetically. "I'd prefer not to, please."
They ate at a beguiling French café, where Frederick had tried Jane to eat snails. She assented rather out of the blue. "I have without exception needed to make it happen," she told him, "since I was a young lady and perused Hans Andersen's account of the white snails who lived in a backwoods of burdocks, and whose case to nobility was that their progenitors had been heated and served in a silver dish."
They had a table in a corner. He requested the lunch meeting skillfully.
"I can't let you know the amount I am appreciating," she said thankfully, as he again offered her his consideration.
"Do you truly like it?"
"Enormously."

"Why not have it until the end of your life?"
Her tone developed. "Here and there I figured it would be — — " she wavered.
"Radiant," he completed the sentence for her. "Jane, you just need to give the signal."
The server, with the main course, hindered them. At the point when he again vanished, Frederick continued. "I'm disappearing to-morrow. Would you offer me my response to-night? After lunch I'll bring you back home and you can rest a little, and afterward I'll come for yourself and we'll feast together and see a play."
She attempted to dissent, however he argued. "This is my day. Try not to over-indulge it, Jane."
It was almost three o'clock when they left the table, and they had a lengthy drive before them. Obscurity had slid when they arrived at the house. It was all the while snowing.
Weave was up-steps, strolling around the little room like a man in a fantasy. "I can't tell you," he confided to Jane after Frederick had left, "how eccentric I felt when I came in and tracked down Miss Martin with the children, and that masterful elderly person in the kitchen. What's more, everything is going predictably. Miss Martin made sense of, and — indeed, Towne simply waves a wand, doesn't he, Janey, and gets things going?"
"I don't realize that I should allow him to accomplish such a great deal," Jane said.

"Gracious, why not, Janey? Simply take the great the divine beings provide...."
Before Frederick Towne arrived at his lodging he passed a shop whose windows were lit against the early murkiness. In one of the windows, flanked by shoes and stockings and a fan to coordinate, was a French outfit, all silver and weak blue, a sparkling wisp of a thing in trim and glossy silk. Towne halted the vehicle, went in and purchased the outfit with its matching embellishments. He conveyed the enormous box with him to his lodging. Resting a piece before supper he allowed himself to dream of Jane in that outfit, the pearls that he would give her against the white of her thin throat, the thin exposed state of her arms, the twirl of a silver ribbon about her lower legs — the swing of the innocent figure in its sheath of blue. He allowed himself to think about her, as well, in different outfits. His contemplations of her dresses were all clear. He had a choice of taste. Assuming he wedded Jane, he would dress her so that individuals would take a gander at her, and look once more. Indeed, even in her destitution, she had figured out how to articulate her thoughts in the things she wore. His cash would make conceivably significantly more inconspicuous articulation.
So he thought about her in dim chiffon, dark pearls in her ears — gracious, to consider Jane in hoops! — with a bit of jade where the curtains swung free — and with a shellfish white coating to the green cape which

would cover the outfit — a lynx collar dependent upon her ears.
Or on the other hand a tea-outfit of tangerine trim — with groups of sable getting the open sleeves at the wrist — or in white — Jane's wedding dress should be weighty with pearls — she loaned herself impeccably to middle age impacts.
His brain returned to blue and silver. It held tight the bed-post, sparkling in the light from his light. He contemplated whether he offered it to Jane, could she acknowledge? He realized she wouldn't. Adelaide would have minced no words about it. There had been something exquisite in dark velvet he had given her, as well, a wrap to coordinate.
Be that as it may, Jane was unique. She would shrug her shoulders and with that beguiling freedom, decline his blessings, shifting her jawline, and testing him with her illuminated eyes. All things considered, he loved her for it. I adored her for it. What's more, sometimes she would wear a blue and silver dress. As he rose and set it back in the case, he appeared to close Jane in with it. There hung about it the aroma of roses. He knew about an uncommon scent. He would arrange a vial of it for Jane. It only indicated scent.
The night extended in front of him, loaded with brilliant commitment. He knew Jane's solidarity yet he was prepared for success.
His phone rang. Furthermore, Jane addressed him.
"Mr. Towne," she said, "I can't eat with you. Be that as it may, could you at

any point come over later? Judy is frantically sick. I'll educate you more when I see you."

## Part XIX

## Give up

Sway had cried when the news came from the medical clinic. It had been loathsome. Jane had never seen a man cry. They had been hard wails, with broken statements of regret between. "I'm numb-skilled to behave like this...."

Jane had attempted to talk, then had sat quiet and awkward while Bob battled for restraint.

Miss Martin had returned home before the message showed up. Sway was informed that he was unable to see his significant other. However, the specialist would absolutely love to converse with him, at eight.

"Furthermore, I understand what he'll say," Bob had shared with Jane grimly, "that on the off chance that I can get that expert up from Hot Springs, he might have the option to analyze the difficulty. Yet, how am I going to get the cash, Janey? It will cost 1,000 bucks to rush him here and pay his charge. What's more, my pay has essentially halted. With every one of these work inconveniences — there's no structure. What's more, Judy's medical caretakers cost twelve bucks every day — and her room five. Gracious, needy individuals haven't any option to be debilitated, Janey. There isn't any spot for them."

Jane's face was pale and looked squeezed. "There's the check Baldy sent me for Christmas, fifty bucks."

"Dear young lady, it wouldn't be a negligible detail."
"I know," mindfully. "Weave, do they imagine that assuming that expert comes it will save Judy's life?"
"It may. It — it's the last opportunity, Janey."
Janey embraced her knees. "Mightn't you at any point get the cash?"
"I have acquired up to the furthest reaches of my protections, and how might I at any point pay?"
Her voice was troubling. "We will figure out how to pay; what presently is to save Judy."
"Indeed," he attempted, miserably, to meet her fortitude. "Assuming they'll get a trained professional, we'll pay."
She had risen. "I'll hit up Mr. Towne, and let him know I can't feast with him."
"In any case, Janey, there's not a great explanation for why you shouldn't keep your commitment."
She had turned on him with a dash of resentment. "How about I have one blissful second with my psyche on Judy?"
Sway had seen her, and afterward turned away. "Have you believed that you could get the cash from Towne?"
Her alarmed look had addressed him. "Get cash from Mr. Towne?"
"Indeed. Gracious, why not, Janey? He'll do anything for you."
"Yet, how is it that I could pay him?"
There had been dead quiet, then Bob said, "All things considered, he's infatuated with you, right?"
"You imply that I would be able — wed him?"

"Indeed. No difference either way. Judy says he's insane regarding you. What's more, Jane, discarding such a chance is stupid. Only one out of every odd young lady has it."
"Be that as it may, Bob, I'm not — in affection with him."
"You'll figure out how to mind — — He's a brilliant chap, I'd say." Bob was energetic. "Presently look here, Janey, I'm conversing with you like a Dutch uncle. Maybe I was encouraging you to do it for the good of us. It is for the wellbeing of your own, as well. Why, it would be perfect, old young lady. Never another concern. Someone generally to take care of you."
The breeze outside was singing a wild tune, a thundering, pessimistic melody, it appeared to Jane. She needed to say to Bob, "However I've forever been cheerful in my little house with Baldy and Philomel, and the chickens and the felines." But obviously Bob could say, "You're troubled now, and at any rate the thing would you say you will do about Judy?"
Judy!
She had finally spoken at work. "I'll advise him to come over after supper. We are a tad."
"Why not stay here? I'll be at the medical clinic. Also, the temperature is quite terrible."
She had watched through the window. "There's no snow. Simply the breeze. What's more, I feel — smothered."
It was then that she had called up Towne. "I can't feast with you.... Judy is frantically ill...."

The house worker had arranged a heavenly supper, yet Jane didn't eat anything. Bounce's hunger, then again, was great. He was sorry for it. "I did without lunch, I was so stressed."
Jane recalled her own lunch — how indiscreet she had been for the occasion, failing to remember her weight of heart — served like a princess shielded from each wind that blew!
And the remainder of her life may be that way! It wouldn't be so awful. She drank some espresso, and afterward another. Furthermore, Frederick had said that he could make her adore him....
In the focal point of the table were a few roses that Towne had given her. She stuck one of them in her support. Sway completed his espresso, and stood up. "I should get going. Best of luck to you, old girl...." His tone was practically bright. He strolled around the table and contacted his lips to her cheek.
At the point when she was separated from everyone else, she went in and checked the children out. Junior had taken a portion of the creatures to bed with him, and they followed over the white cover — little tigers and elephants, lions and giraffes. Little Julia embraced her doll. How sweet she was, and such a child!
What's more, in the clinic Judy's arms longed to enclose that warm little body: Judy's heart beat with dread in case they ought to at absolutely no point ever envelop her in the future!

The chime rang. Jane, going to the entryway, ended up shaking with energy.
Frederick came in and took both of her hands in his. "Please accept my apologies about my sister. Is there anything I can do?"
She shook her head. She could hardly speak. “I thought if you wouldn’t mind, we’d go for a ride. And we can talk.”
“Good. Get your wraps.” He released her hands, and she went into the other room. As she looked into the mirror she saw that her cheeks were crimson.
She brought out her coat and he held it for her. “Is this warm enough? You ought to have a fur coat.”
“Oh, I shall be warm,” she said.
As he preceded her down the stairs, Towne turned and looked up at her. “You are wearing my rose,” he told her, ardently; “you are like a rose yourself.”
She would not have been a woman if she had not liked his admiration. And he was strong and adoring and distinguished. She had a sense of almost happy excitement as he lifted her into the car.
“Where shall we drive?” he asked.
“Along the lake. I love it on a night like this.”
The moon was sailing high in a rack of clouds. As they came to the lake the waves writhed like mad sea-monsters in gold and white and black.
“Jane,” Frederick asked softly, “what made you wear—my rose?”
She sat very still beside him. “Mr. Towne,” she said at last, “tell me how much—you love me.”

He gave me a start of surprise. Then he turned towards her and took her hand in his. “Let me tell you this! there never was a dearer woman. Everything that I have, all that I am, is yours if you will have it.”

There was a fine dignity in his avowal. She liked him more than ever.

“Do you love me enough”—she hurried over the words, “to help me?”

“Yes.” He drew her gently towards him. There was no struggle. She lay quietly against his arm, but he was aware that she trembled.

“Mr. Towne, Judy must have a great specialist right away. It’s her only chance. If you will send for him to-night, make yourself responsible for—everything—I’ll marry you whenever you say.”

He stared down at her, unbelieving.

“Do you mean it, Jane?”

“Yes. Oh, do you think I am dreadful?”

He laughed exultantly, catching her up to him. “Dreadful? You’re the dearest—ever, Jane.”

Yet as he felt her fluttering heart, he released her gently. Her eyes were full of tears. He touched her wet cheek.

“Don’t let me frighten you, my dear. But I am very happy.”

She believed herself happy. He was really—irresistible. A conqueror. Yet always with that touch of deference.

“Do you love me, Jane?”

“Not—yet.”

“But you will. I’ll make you love me.”

With keen intuition, with his knowledge, too, of women, he asked for no further assurance. He leaned back against the cushions of the car, and holding her hand in his, made

plans for their future. He will get the ring to-morrow. He will come again in a week. As soon as Judy was better, he and Jane would be married.
Then just before they reached home he asked for the rose. She gave it to him, all fading fragrance. He touched it to her lips then crushed it against his own.
"Must I be content with this?"
Her quick breath told her agitation. He drew her to him, gently. "Come, my sweet."
Oh, money, money. Jane learned that night the power of it!
Coming in with Frederick from that wild moonlighted world, flushed with excitement, hardly knowing this new Jane, she saw Bob transformed in a moment from haggard hopelessness to wild elation.
Frederick Towne had made a simple statement. "Jane has told me how serious things are, Heming. I want to help." Then he had asked for the surgeon's name; spoken at once of a change of rooms for Judy; increased attendance. There was much telephoning and telegraphing. An atmosphere of efficiency. Jane, looking on, was filled with admiration. How well he did things. And someday he will be her husband!
Towne was, indeed, at his best. Deeply in love with her, all his generous impulses were quickened for her service. When at last he had gone, she went to bed, and lay awake almost until morning. Doubts crowded upon her. Her cheeks burned as she thought of the bargain she had made. He would pay her sister's bills—and

she would marry him. But it wasn't just that! He was so tender, so solicitous. Jane had not yet learned that one may be in love with being loved, which is not in the least the same as loving. Against the benefits which Towne bestowed upon her, she could set only her dreams of Galahad, of Robin Hood! Of romantic adventure! Her memories—of Evans Follette.

She sighed as she thought of him. He would be unhappy. Oh, darling old Evans! She cried a little into her pillow. She mustn't think of him. The thing was done. She was going to marry Frederick Towne!

## CHAPTER XXI

## VOICES IN THE DARK

Arthur Lane and Sandy talked it over.

"I wonder what has happened. He looks dreadful."

The two boys were on their way to Castle Manor. They wanted books. Evans' library was a treasure-house for youthful readers. It had all the old adventuring tales. And Evans had read everything. He would simply walk up to a shelf, lay his hand on a book, and say, "Here's one you'll like." And he was never wrong.

He had told them that the latch-string was always out for them. And they had learned to look for his welcome. Sometimes he asked them to stay, and phoned their parents. And then they popped corn before the library fire, or made taffy in the kitchen. And sometimes Baldy Barnes was there and that wonderful Miss Towne. And Mrs. Follette. The boys didn't care in the least what the rest of Sherwood thought about Mrs. Follette. They liked her and when she made the taffy and stood over the boiling kettle with the big spoon in her hand, they thought her regal in spite of the humble nature of her occupation.

But of late, Evans Follette had met them with an effort. “Look for yourselves,” he had said, when they asked for books, and sat staring into the fire. And he had not urged them to stay. His manner had been kind but inattentive. They were puzzled and a little hurt. “I feel sorta queer when he acts that way,” Sandy was saying, “as if he didn’t take any interest. I don’t even know whether he wants us any more.”

Arthur refused to believe his hero inhospitable. “It’s just that he’s got things on his mind.”

They reached the house and rang the bell. Old Mary let them in. “He’s in the library,” she said, and they went towards it. The door was open and they entered. But the room was empty....

That morning Baldy had had a letter from Jane and had handed it to Evans. It was the first long letter since her engagement to Towne. Baldy had written to his sister, flamingly, demanding to know if she was really happy. And she had said:

“I shall be when Judy is better. That is all I can think of just now. Her life is hanging in the balance. We can never be thankful enough that we got the specialist when we did. He had found the trouble. The question now is whether she will have the strength for another operation. When she gets through with that! Well, then I’ll talk to you, darling. I hardly know how I feel. The days are so whirling. Mr. Towne has been more than generous. If the little I can give him will repay him, then I must give it, dearest. And it won't be hard. He is so very good to me."

And now this letter had come after Towne's second visit:

"Baldy, dear, I am very happy. And I want you to set your mind at rest. I am not marrying Mr. Towne for what he has done for us all, but because I love him. Please believe it. You can't understand what he has been to me in these dark days. I have learned to know how kind he is—and how strong. I haven't a care in the world when he is here, and everything is so—marvelous. You should see my ring—a great sapphire, Baldy, in a square of diamonds. He is crazy to buy things for me, but I won't let him. I will take things for Judy but not for myself. You can see that, of course. I just go everywhere with him in my cheap little frocks, to the theaters and to all the great restaurants, and we have the most delectable things to eat. It is really great fun.

"Judy is so happy over the whole thing, that it is helping her to get well. She says she was half afraid to advise me, but she knew it was for my happiness. Bob simply walks on air. He says when business grows better, he will pay back every cent to Mr. Towne. And of course he must. But none of us have been made to feel that we ought to be grateful. Mr. Towne says that he simply held out a friendly hand when we needed it, and that's all there is to it.

"Well, dearest dear, I wish I could hear Philomel sing o' mornings, and see Merrymaid and the kit-cat on the hearth, but best of all would be to have your own darling self on the other side of the table."

Since he had heard the news of Jane's approaching marriage, Evans had lived in a dream. The people about him had shadow-shapes. He had walked and talked with them, remembering nothing afterward but his great weariness. He had eaten his meals at stated times, and had not known what he was eating. He had gone to his office, and behind closed doors had sat at his desk, staring. Nothing mattered. All incentive was gone. He spoke of Jane to no one. Not even to his mother. He had a morbid horror of hearing her name. When he came across anything that reminded him of her, he suffered actual physical pain.

And now this letter! "You see what she says," Baldy had raged. "Of course she isn't in love with him. But she thinks she is. There's nothing more that I can do."

Evans had taken the letter to the library to read. He was alone, except for Rusty, who had limped after him and laid at his feet.

She loved—Towne. And that settled it. "I am marrying Mr. Towne because I love him." Nothing could be plainer than that. Baldy might protest. But the words were there.

As Evans sat gazing into the fire, he saw her as she had so often been in this old room—as a child, sprawled on the hearth-rug over some entrancing book from his shelves, swinging her feet on the edge of a table while he bragged of his athletic prowess; leaning over war-maps, while he pointed out the fields of fighting; curled up in a corner on the couch while he read to her—"Oh, silver shrine, here will I take my rest...."

He could no longer stand his thoughts. Without a hat or heavy coat, he stepped through one of the long windows and into the night.

As he walked on in the darkness, he had no knowledge of his destination. He swept on and on, pursued by dreadful thoughts.

On and on through the blackness.... No moon ... a wet wind blowing ... on and on....

He came to a scaffold which crossed a course. No water streamed under it. However, not too far off which drove through the Glen was another extension, and underneath it a profound, still pool.

With the possibility of that profound and calm pool came flitting help from the repulsions which had dogged him. It would be simple. A subsequent battle. Then, at that point, everything was over. Harmony. No feelings of trepidation. No fear of the future....

It appeared to be quite a while later, that, resting up against the support of the scaffold, he heard, with expanding clearness, young men's voices in obscurity.

He moved back among the shadows. It was Sandy and Arthur. Not three feet from him — passing.

"Indeed, obviously, Mr. Follette is only a man," Sandy was saying.

"Perhaps he is," Arthur said truly, "yet I don't have the foggiest idea. Something really doesn't add up about him — — "

He stopped.

"Go on," Sandy encouraged.

"All things considered, something" — Arthur was battling to articulate his thoughts, "stunning. It focuses like a light — — "

Their lively strides left the extension, and were dulled by the back road past. Sandy's reaction was quiet. A last mumble, and afterward quiet. Evans was cleared by a flood of feeling; his heart, warm and alive, started to pulsate where there had been a frozen vacancy.

"Something awe inspiring — that focuses like a light!"

Years later he discussed this second to Jane. "I can't portray it. It was a marvel — their coming. As a very remarkable marvel as that light which gleamed on Paul as he rode to Damascus. The change inside me was outright. I was brought back to life. Every one of the old feelings of trepidation slipped from me like a piece of clothing. I was saved, Jane, by those young men's voices in obscurity."

The following day was Sunday. Evans called up Sandy and Arthur and welcomed them to dinner. "Old Mary said you were here the previous evening, and didn't track down me. I've a book or two for you. Could you at any point come and get them? Also, remain for dinner. Miss Towne will be here with her uncle."

The young men couldn't realize that they were asked as a safeguard and buckler in the fight which Evans was battling. He couldn't help suspecting that he was unable to meet Frederick Towne. However it had been, obviously, the intelligent thing to ask him. Edith had welcomed herself, and Towne had, obviously, much to tell about Jane.

Evans, hence, with an outward impact of serenity, played the host. After dinner, be that as it may, he took the young men with him to the library. On the table lay a dim volume. He opened it and showed the Cruikshank outlines.

"I've been understanding this. It's incredible stuff."

"Gracious, Pilgrim's Progress," said Sandy; "do you like it?"

"Indeed." Evans inclined over the book where it is exposed under the light. "Tune in:

"'Then Apollyon, espying his chance, started to get together near Christian, and grappling with him, gave him an unpleasant fall: and with that, Christian's blade flew out of his hand. Then said Apollyon, I am certain of you now: and with that, he had nearly beaten him to death, so Christian started to surrender all expectations regarding life. Be that as it may, as God would have it, while Apollyon was bringing of his last blow, subsequently to make a full finish of this great Man, Christian deftly connected his hand for his Sword, and got it, saying, Rejoice not against me, O mine Enemy! at the point when I fall, I will emerge: and with that, gave him a lethal push, which made him offer in return, as one that had accepted his human injury: that's what christian seeing, made at him again saying, Nay, in everything we are more than Conquerors, through him that cherished us. Furthermore, with that, Apollyon spread forward his Dragon's wings, and sped him away, that Christian saw him no more.'"

Evans' ringing voice gave full worth to the words. It appeared to Arthur, loving his legend, as though he flung a heaved disobedience at some concealed enemy — "Cheer not against me, O mine Enemy! at the point when I fall, I will emerge!"

However when he turned upward from the book Evans' eyes were grinning. "Might you want to bring it back home with you? It is an uncommon version, yet you know how to deal with it. Furthermore, I might want to have you understand it. Some time or another you might meet Apollyon. What's more, I may think that it is useful. As I have."

Later as the young men headed back home together, the valuable volume under Arthur's arm, Sandy said, "He's more like himself, right? More kicks."

"I'll say he is," however Arthur was not fulfilled. "I wish he'd let us know what he implied when he discussed gathering Apollyon."

That evening Evans found out something interesting about his mom. "You look drained, dearest," he had said, when their visitors were gone, and he and she had come into the extraordinary lobby together.

"I'm worn out." She plunked down on an old horsehair couch. "I can't handle a lot of energy. It causes me to feel like an old woman."

"You won't ever become old." He felt a profound delicacy for her at this time of admitted shortcoming. She had forever been an area of strength for so. Had would not incline. She had, truth be told, taken from him his child's right of defense.

He laid his hand on her shoulder. "You would be wise to see Hallam."

"I've seen him."

"What did he say?"

"My heart — — "

He saw her in caution. "Mother! For what reason didn't you tell me?"

"What was the utilization? All in all nothing remains to be stressed over. Just he says I should not propel myself."

"I'm stressed. Allow me to care for the men in the first part of the day early. That will give you an additional rest."

"Goodness, I will not make it happen, Evans. You have your work."

"It won't hurt me. Furthermore, I will manage you around a little." He stooped and kissed her. "You are too valuable to even consider losing, Mumsie."

She gripped him. "What might I manage without you, my dear?"

He helped her up the steps. Furthermore, as she climbed gradually, his arm about her, he thought about that dim second by the extension.

On the off chance that those youthful voices had not come to him in the evening, this caring soul could have been blasted and made ruined; abandoned in her period of most prominent scarcity.

Section XXII

AT THE OLD INN

Again the Washington papers had titles that discussed Delafield Simms. He had hitched a transcriber in Frederick Towne's office. Furthermore, it was Towne's niece that he had abandoned at the special raised area. What's more, generally astounding of all, Edith Towne had been at the wedding. It was Eloise Harper who told the columnists.

"They were hitched at the old Inn beneath Alexandria earlier today, by the neighborhood Methodist minister. Miss Logan is a Methodist — extravagant. What's more, Edith was a bridesmaid."

Yet, Eloise didn't realize that Lucy had worn the wedding dress and shroud that Edith had given her and looked exquisite in them. Furthermore, after the function, Delafield had wrung Edith's hand and had said, "I won't ever know how to thank you for what you have been to Lucy."

Edith's real to life eyes had met him decisively. "You realize you are not half sufficient for her, Del," and he had said, modestly, "I'm not and that is reality. However, I will do my best to be what she thinks I am."

Martha and her better half had served a flavorful breakfast in the huge void lounge area. Just Edith and Baldy were there other than the lady of the hour and lucky man. Lucy reasonably wouldn't have any pomp and circumstance. "Assuming it hushes up, individuals will not have such a great amount to say regarding it."

Delafield's way to Lucy was great. "What do you think she has made me do?" he asked Edith. "Purchase a homestead in Virginia. We will raise pigs — dark Berkshires, since Lucy enjoys the inclination of their ears and the twist of their tails. She has been perusing books about them, and we will spend our special night motoring around the nation and purchasing stock."

Gracious, bravo, bravo, little Lucy, not to take a chance with exhausting this trendy youthful spouse with a regular wedding trip! Edith needed to applaud. Yet, she made no sign, but to meet Lucy's calm look with a lift of the eyebrows.

Edith and Baldy waited after the lady and lucky man had driven off in an extraordinarily dark vehicle — destined for the Virginia country place which Delafield had purchased, and prepared for the inhabitants in the sparkling of an eye.

"Well, however you're a standout," Baldy told her as they strolled in the nursery.

"Am I?"

"Indeed. Furthermore, the manner in which you took it away."

"I didn't cart it away. It held itself."

"Is it true or not that you are certain it didn't do any harm?"

She grinned at him from underneath her huge cap. "Not at all."

The container supports in the nursery were showing a smidgen of new green. There was a plum tree blossoming rashly. The sun made earthy colored shadows along the stream's edge, and the wash of the waves from passing liners went lip-lapping among the reeds and surges. The second was ready for sentiment. Be that as it may, Baldy hotly got the discussion far from serious things. They had talked truly enough, God knew, a few evenings ago by Edith's fire. He had seen her forlorn in the prospect of her future.

"At the point when Uncle Fred weds I won't remain here."

He had longed to take her in his arms, to tell her that against his heart she ought to at absolutely no point in the future know depression. In any case, he had not tried. What brought him to the table? A kid's affection. Against her gold.

He told himself with some sharpness that one fortune was sufficient in a family. Jane's commitment had changed things for her sibling. The hostility which Baldy had consistently felt for Frederick was heightened. The prospect of Towne's cash weighed intensely upon him. Jane had proactively set herself under insuperable commitments. Regardless of whether she wished, she couldn't currently shake herself free.

What's more, Edith's cash? He and Jane living on the Towne millions? He wouldn't have it.

So he discussed Jane. "She doesn't need her commitment reported until she gets back. I believe she's right."

"I don't," Edith said lethargically. "If I cherished a man I'd need to yell it to the world."

They were perched on a natural seat under the blooming plum tree. Edith's hands were caught behind her head, and the winged sleeves of her outfit fell back and showed her exposed arms. Baldy needed to unclasp those hands, smash them to his lips — however rather he stood up, investigating the waterway.

"Do you see the ducks out there? Wild ones at that. It's an indication of spring."

She rose and remained alongside him. "Furthermore, you can discuss — ducks — on a day like this?"

"Indeed," he didn't see her, "ducks are — safe."

He heard her low chuckle. "Senseless kid."

He turned, his dim eyes loaded up with clear light. "Maybe I am. Be that as it may, I ought to be a nitwit assuming I let you know how I love you. Love you. You know it, obviously. Yet, nothing can happen to it, regardless of whether I were sufficiently arrogant to believe that you — care."

She cleared out her hands in an engaging motion. "Let's assume it. I need to hear."

She was charming. Yet, he stepped back a bit. "We've gone excessively far and excessively quickly. It is my shortcoming, obviously, for being a heartfelt nitwit."

"I'm worried we're a couple of heartfelt blockheads, Baldy."

He turned and put his hands on her shoulders. "Edith, I — mustn't."

"What difference would it make?"

"Not until I bring something to the table for you — — "
"You bring something to the table — — "
"Gracious, I understand what you mean. However, — I will not. Some way or another this issue of Jane's with your uncle has made me see — — "
"See what?"
"Goodness, how the world would check it out. He'd's perspective."
"Uncle Frederick? He hasn't a thing to do with it. I'm my own courtesan."
"I know. However, — — Oh, I can't dissect it, Edith. I love you — no closure. More than — anything. In any case, I will not request that you wed me."
"Do you have at least some idea how childish you are?"
"I know how wise I am."
She made an eager signal. "You're not considering me at all. You are thinking about your pride."
He got her hand in his. "I'm thinking about my pride. Do you guess it is simple for me to let Jane — take cash from him? To feel that there is no man in our family who can take care of the bills? I'm pleased. Furthermore, I'm happy about it. Edith — I believe that you should be happy that I won't take — aid."
Her shrewd eyes read him briefly. "You favored kids. You favored writer," she murmured, "I'm glad for you, however my heart throbs — for myself."
He got her generally in his arms and in a second delivered her. "I'm correct, dearest?"

"No, you're not right. On the off chance that we wedded, we'd sail to Italy and have a manor by the ocean. Also, you would paint show-stoppers. Do you suppose my cash counts next to your ability? All things considered, I don't."
"My dear, let me demonstrate my ability first. As things are presently, I was unable to pay our section to the opposite side."
"You could. My cash would be yours — your ability mine. A fair trade."
He adhered unyieldingly to his perspective. "I won't attach you to any commitment until I've shown what I can do."
"Also, we'll lose this multitude of sparkling years."
"We will not lose a second. I will work for you."
He was, she saw, on the levels. Yet, she knew the exhaustion of the ascension.
Emerging from the nursery in the late evening, they knew about different landings in the Inn.
"Adelaide and Uncle Fred, by every one of the divine beings," said Edith, as they looked into the lounge area from the obscurity of the lobby.
"Gracious, don't allow them to see us. Adelaide's such a bromide."
They crawled out, tracked down Baldy's vehicle and sped towards the city. "I ought to say," Baldy broadcast harshly, "that for a draw in, a man is locked in, a thing like that is unspeakable."
"Goodness, Uncle Fred and Adelaide," said Edith, without any problem; "she presumably asked him. Furthermore,

she was mournful. A sad lady generally gets everything she could possibly want."
Adelaide had been mournful. What's more, she had indicated for the ride.
"Why not a midday ride, Ricky? It will rest you."
"Sorry. In any case, I'm restricted."
"I haven't seen you for a long time, Ricky."
"I know, old young lady. I've had 1,000 things."
"I've — missed you."
It was difficult for Frederick to overlook that. Adelaide was an appealing lady.
"No matter. I can move away at four. We'll have tea at the old Inn."
"Magnificent. Ricky, I have another blue cap."
"You could constantly sport blue." He concluded that he should make things lovely. There was a shock coming up for her. Obviously he'd need to inform her concerning Jane.
So Adelaide in the new blue cap — with a wrap that coordinated — with that porcelain white and pink of her composition — with her delicate voice, and engaging way, had Frederick for three entire hours to herself.
She let him know all the fiery tattle. Frederick, as most men, apparently despised embarrassment, yet listened attentively. What Eloise had said, what Benny had said, what all the world was talking about Del's marriage.
"Furthermore, they were hitched here to-day. I didn't dream it until Eloise hit me up not long before lunch. Edith had told her."
"Edith was here?"
"Indeed, and youthful Barnes."

She halted there and poured the tea. She did it nimbly, however Frederick's contemplations cleared back to Jane behind her parapets of silver.
"Four irregularities, Ricky?"
"Um — yes."
"Curious what you might be thinking."
"They're worthless, Adelaide. Loads of lemon, please. What's more, no cakes. I'm attempting to keep my wonderful figure."
"Goodness, why stress? I like enormous men."
"That is decent of you."
Martha's little wipe cakes were light as a quill. Adelaide broke one and ate gently. Then she said, "How's little Jane Barnes?"
Frederick was quickly reluctant. "She's still in Chicago."
"Sister better?"
"Much."
"When is she returning?"
"Jane? In a hurry as Mrs. Heming can be brought back. In half a month, I trust."
Adelaide drank some tea nearly at a draft. She knew about a looming divulgence. At the point when the blow came, she took it without the glint of an eyelash.
"I will wed Jane Barnes, Adelaide. The commitment isn't to be reported until she gets back to Washington. However, I believe my companions should be aware."
She put her elbows on the table, fastened her hands and laid her jawline on them checking out at him with watchful gazes. "So that is its finish, Ricky?"
"The finish of what?"

"Our companionship."
"For what reason would it be advisable for it to be?"
"Gracious, do you imagine that your little Jane will allow you to philander?"
"I don't have any desire to philander. Assuming that is the manner in which you put it."
"So you believe you're in — love with her."
"I realize I am," the red came up in his cheeks, yet he adhered to it manfully. "It's unique in relation to anything — ever that I've felt previously."
"They all say that, don't they, like clockwork?"
"Try not to be so — critical."
She shrugged her shoulders. "I'm not. All things considered, I will miss you, Ricky, dear."
That was all, simply that sad note. However, Adelaide's mournfulness was dependably successful.
So after tea they strolled in the nursery, and sat under the plum tree, and watched out upon the stream — where the shadows were rose-red in the sunset, and Adelaide said, "My life is that way — my sun has set."
Frederick connected a thoughtful hand. "Try not to say that, old young lady."
Adelaide lifted his hand to her cheek. "This is truly 'farewell,' isn't it, Ricky? It appears to be somewhat eccentric to say it."

## Part XXIV

## Tormented

It was after the day when she had met Evans in the Glen that Jane started to be spooky by apparitions.

There was a phantom who meandered through Sherwood on moonlights, a limping, delaying apparition who said, "You're wine, Jane. I should have my day to day taste of you."
Furthermore, there was a phantom who arrived dazed and said, "You are a lamp, Jane — held high."
Furthermore, that apparition in the shine of the hearth-fire — "You are food and drink to me, Jane. Do you know it?"
Apparitions, phantoms, phantoms; holding out engaging hands to her. What's more, she was consistently dismissed. However, presently she didn't turn. Again and again she listened carefully to those murmuring words, "Jane, you are wine.... Jane, you are a lantern.... You are food and drink, Jane...."
Indeed, she was having her discipline. She had not cherished him when he wanted her. What's more, now that she really wanted him, she should not cherish him.
She barely knew herself. Every one of the long stretches of her life she had seen things straight, and she had attempted to satisfy that vision. She saw them straight at this point. She didn't adore Frederick Towne. She reserved no option to wed him. However she should. There was no chance to get out.
Towne knew about a distinction in her when he got back from New York. She was more remote. Somewhat less responsive. However these things caused him no uneasiness. Her fresh coolness had consistently comprised one of her incredible charms. "You are

worn out, dearest," he told her. "I wish you would wed me immediately, and let me satisfy you."

They were eating at the Capitol in the Senate café. Frederick was an impressive figure and Jane knew about his significance. Individuals looked at him and looked once more, and afterward let others know what his identity was. Sometimes she would be his significant other, and everyone would be telling every other person that she was the spouse of the incomparable Frederick Towne.

The mindful server at her elbow laid toast on her plate, and served Maryland crab from a silver scraping dish. Frederick understood what she loved and had requested without asking her. In any case, the delightful food was bland. She had been apprehensive that Frederick would agree to something about a quick marriage, and presently he was saying it.

"Gracious," she told him, sincerely, "you guaranteed I could hold on until Judy could come on. In June."

"I know. Be that as it may, it will be extremely hot, and you'll have an entire lifetime to see Judy."

"Be that as it may, not at my wedding. She's my main sister."

"I see," yet his voice showed his disturbance; "however maybe your family has requested enough of you. Might you at any point contemplate yourself — and me?"

She squeezed her point. "Judy resembles my mom. I can't be hitched without her and the children."

"On the off chance that the infants come, you'll be taking care of them as late as possible, and it will be an incredible stress on you, darling."
"Goodness, it will not be. I love children."
His fast desire erupted. "I don't," he said, with a dash of money. "I'm not attached to kids."
She ate peacefully. What's more, he said contritely, "You should think of me as an extraordinary animal, Jane. Yet, you don't have the foggiest idea what lengths I will go for you."
He resembled a contrite kid. She made herself grin at him. "I think you are extremely quiet, Mr. Towne."
"I'm not patient. I'm generally eager. What's more, when are you going to quit calling me Mr. Towne?"
"At the point when I can call you — spouse."
"Be that as it may, I would rather not hold on up to that point, dearest."
"Yet, 'Frederick' is so lengthy, and 'Fred' is so short, and 'Ricky' seems like a highball." She had lost her downturn and was shining.
"No one calls me 'Ricky' except for Adelaide. I generally couldn't stand it."
"Did you?" She was coy. "I could say 'my affection,' like the women in the dated books."
He chuckled delightedly. "Let's assume it."
She submitted startlingly. "My affection, we are welcome to seven days end with the Delafield Simms, at their new nation place, Grass Hills."
"Are we?" Then in an unexpected fervent hurry of words, "Jane, I'd kiss

you on the off chance that the world wasn't looking on."
"The columnists would be happy. Titles."
"I'm worn out on titles. Also, what do you mean about going to Delafield Simms?"
"They are requesting a ton from his companions. It is his significant first experience with his old group. Much will rely upon whether you and Edith will acknowledge. Furthermore, it was Edith who asked me to — make you come — — "
She gave him reality, realizing that it generally will be preferable over strategy. "I told her that I was unable to make you. Be that as it may, maybe assuming you realized I needed it — — " She stopped inquiringly.
He inclined towards her across the table. "Ask me, agreeably, and I'll do it."
"Truly?" She snickered, became flushed and did it. "Will you go — my adoration?"
"Might I at any point deny that?" He emanated fulfillment. "Do you have any idea about how beguiling you are, Jane?"
"Am I? However, it is decent of you to go. I realize how you can't stand it."
"Not assuming you are there. Also, presently, who else is inquired?"
"Goodness, Mrs. Laramore and Eloise Harper and a ton of others. Lucy says she'll be totally out of place, yet Delafield has decided that his companions shouldn't imagine that he's embarrassed about her."
At the point when their frosts came and their espresso, Frederick said, "I

must spend a half-hour in a boardroom. Will I take you up to the Senate Gallery?"
"No — there's nothing intriguing, is there? I'll stand by Statuary Hall."
Jane adored the marble calculates that orbited the Hall. Quite a while back there had not been so many. They had been, then, at that point, maybe, more particular. As a youngster, she had picked as her top choices the pleasant Colonials, the frontiersmen in calfskin tunics and coonskin covers. She had never enjoyed the legislators in solid shirts and dress coats, despite the fact that she had conceded their ethics. Indeed, even the ambiguous exemplary curtains were more with regards to the allure which the past flung over the ones who had done everything they could for America. Be that as it may, it was Fulton who had caught her creative mind, with his little boat, and Pere Marquette with his cross, the harmony adoring Quaker who had vanquished; globe-trotter, trailblazer, cleric and prophet — developers all of the construction of the new world.
She considered what people in the future would add to this sublime organization. Could the Anglo-Saxon give way to the Semite? Could the Huguenot respect the Slav? Also, could these novices hold high the flag of public optimism? What might they give? Also, what might they remove?
There were gatherings of tourists assembled about the extraordinary room — an aide putting them to a great extent on the marble blocks. The

stunt was to put somebody behind a mottled support point far away, and allow him to talk. Inferable from some odd acoustic quality the sound would be called to the individual who remained on the murmuring stone.

A long time back Jane had tuned in while a voice had come reverberating across the empty spaces of the incomparable Hall, "My nation — right or wrong — my nation — — "

Another phantom! The phantom of a kid, energetic, enthusiastically dedicated to the incredible old divine beings. "Obviously they were just men, Jane. Humans. Broken. Be that as it may, they bursted a way of opportunity for the individuals who followed...."

At the point when Frederick came, he tracked down her remains before the tidy sculpture of Frances Willard.

"Worn out, darling?"

"No."

"I remained longer than I anticipated."

"It didn't appear to be long. I have had a lot of organization."

He was perplexed. "Your meaning could be a little more obvious."

"Every one of these." Her hand showed the marble people.

He snickered. "Extraordinary old oddities, right?"

Monstrosities!

Divine beings!

Indeed, obviously, everything relied totally upon the perspective.

"I like them all," she said, sturdily, "even the ones in the terrible gown coats."

"Most likely not, my dear."

"Indeed, I do. They might have terrible workmanship, however they're great Americans."
His chuckle was liberal. "After you've been abroad a couple of times, you will not be so common."
"In the event that being common means adoring my own, I'll remain commonplace."
"Travel expands the psyche, changes the perspective."
"Yet, for what reason would it be a good idea for me to cherish my nation less? I know her flaws. Also, I know Baldy's. However, I love him regardless."
As they strolled on, he fell into step with her. "We won't contend. You are presumably correct, and on the off chance that not, you're excessively beautiful for me to go against."
His heroism was impeccable, yet she needed more than bravery. There had been a clear compromise of her contentions with Evans. They had regal fights, youth had challenged youth. What's more, from their conflicts had come convictions.
Yet again she had the deception of Frederick as a plume pad! He would maybe concur with her generally! Furthermore, her spirit would be — covered!

## Part XXVI
## THE DISCORDANT NOTE

Lucy was still to Eloise Harper the transcription of Frederick Towne. Awkward, obviously, in this fine ranch style home, with its proper nurseries, its extraordinary corrals, its entourage of workers.

"How would you manage yourselves?" she asked her lady, as she descended, prepared for supper, in uncovering apricot curtains and found Lucy fresh in white organdie with a band of dark velvet around her throat.
"Do?" Lucy's grin was open. "We are exceptionally occupied, Del and I. We feed the pigs."
"Pigs?" Eloise gazed. She had expected that a young lady of Lucy's sort would influence an intricate mentality of relaxation. Also, she was right here, all things being equal, stylishly enthusiastic.
They took care of the pigs, it appeared, as a matter of fact.
"Obviously not the huge ones. However, the little ones have their jugs. There are ten and their mom passed on. You ought to see Del and me. He conveys the jug in a metal holder — round," — Lucy's hand depicts the shape, — "and when they see him coming they all screech, and it's charming."
Lucy's air was coy. She was exceptionally cheerful. She was a lady of solid soul. As of now she had intrigued her frail spouse past anything he had at any point known in his floating long stretches of bachelorhood. "After supper," she told Eloise, "I'll show you Del's roses. They are very glorious. I figure his assortment will be past anything in this piece of the country."
Delafield, coming up, said, "They are Lucy's roses, however she says I am to accomplish the work."
"However, why not have a landscaper?" Eloise requested.

"Gracious, we have. However, I ought to hate to have our nursery a simple matter of — mechanics. Del has a few marvelous thoughts. We will work for the blossom shows. Prizes what not." Delafield murmured like a feline. "I will name my most memorable rose the 'Little Lucy Logan.'"

Edith, locking arms with Jane, somewhat later, as they walked around a wisteria-draped lattice towards the wellspring, said, "Lucy's making a man of him since she cherishes him. Also, I would have chuckled at him. We would have exhausted one another."

"They won't ever be exhausted," Jane chose, "with their roses and their little pigs."

They had arrived at the wellspring. It was a dated one, with slim floods of water rambling up from the bill of a tanned crane. There were goldfish in the pool, and a major green frog jumped from a lily cushion. Past the wellspring the wisteria roofed a way of pale light. A peacock strolled gradually towards them, its long tail clearing the ground in shined excellence.

"Consider this," said Jane, "and Lucy's days at the workplace."

"But then," Edith contemplated, "she told me on the off chance that if he had not had a penny she would have been content with him."

"I trust it. With a cabin, one pig, and a flower hedge, they would track down rapture. It is like that with them."

The two ladies plunked down on the marble adaptation of the wellspring. The peacock followed by them, its gems generally burning under the sun.

"That peacock makes me consider Adelaide." Edith cleared her hand through the water, frightening the little fishes.
"Why?"
"In that dress she had on to-night — bronze and blue and green tulle. I will express this for Adelaide, she knows how to dress."
"Does she at any point consider something else yet garments?"
"Men," briefly.
"Gracious."
"Ladies like Adelaide," Edith explained, "need to look well, and to be respected. They live for it. They get up in the first part of the day and head to sleep with that one thought. What's more, the men get bulldozed."
"Isn't that right?"
"Indeed. Adelaide knows how to play on the keys of their vanity. You and I don't — or will not. At the point when our childhood goes, Jane, we'll be cherished for our temperances. Adelaide will be adored for the part she plays, and she plays it well."
She snickered and stood up. "I'm apprehensive that your declaration to-morrow will put her in a terrible mood, Jane."
"She knows," Jane said unobtrusively. "Mr. Towne told her."
"Truly?" Edith halted, and happened in an ease off volume, "Discussing holy messengers — here she comes."
Adelaide, in her shined tulle, tall, thin, smooth as a willow, was swinging along underneath the lattice. The peacock had turned and strolled alongside her. "What an image Baldy

could think about that," Edith said, "'The Proud Lady.'"

"Do you know," Jane's voice was likewise brought down, "when I take a gander at her, I feel that she ought to wed your uncle."

Edith was honest. "I can't stand her. Thus would he in a month. She's fake, and you are so delightfully regular, Jane."

Adelaide had arrived at the circle of light that encompassed the wellspring. "The men have come and have gone up to dress," she said. "All with the exception of your uncle, Edith. He said that he couldn't arrive until after supper. He has a significant gathering."

"He said he may be late. Benny came, obviously?"

"Indeed, Eloise is cheerful. He had brought her all the town tattle. That is the reason I left. I can't stand tattle."

Edith knew that posture. Nobody could talk more devastatingly than Adelaide of her neighbor's undertakings. However, she did it, unobtrusively, with an impact of noble cause. "I'm exceptionally partial to her," was her approach to introducing a savage disclosure.

"I figured your sibling would be down," Adelaide took a gander at Jane, balanced on the edge of the wellspring, similar to a blue butterfly, — "however he wasn't with the rest."

"Baldy can't be here until to-morrow early afternoon. He must be in the workplace."

"How are you going to manage yourself meanwhile, Edith?" Adelaide was in a mind-set to make individuals self-conscious. She was awkward herself. Jane, in surging glorious blue with rose strips drifting at her support, was youth in bodily form. What's more, it was her childhood that had drawn in Towne.

The three ladies strolled towards the house together. As they emerged from under the arbor, they knew about dark mists extended across the skyline. "I trust it won't rain," Edith said. "Lucy is intending to serve supper on the patio."

Adelaide was peevish. "I wish she wouldn't. There'll be bugs and things."

Jane preferred the possibility of an out-of-entryway supper. She believed that the house keepers in their pink material were like rose-leaves blown across the grass. There was an incredible umbrella over the table, rose-striped. "How gay it is," she said; "I trust the downpour won't over-indulge it."

At the point when they arrived at the wide-pillared piazza, nobody was there. The breeze was blowing consistently from the bank of mists. Edith went in to get a scarf.

Thus Jane and Adelaide were let be. Adelaide sat in a major seat with a back like a spreading fan; she was graceful, and knew it, however she would have traded right now every exemplary line for the impact that Jane gave of unpremeditated elegance and excellence. The youngster had flung a pad on the marble step, and had dropped downward on it. The breeze made up for lost time her unsettles, so she appeared to drift in a cloud.

She giggled, and tucked her spinning curtains about her. "I love the breeze, don't you?"
Adelaide didn't cherish the breeze. It messed up her hair. She felt angrily prepared to hurt Jane.
"It is a pity," she said, after stopping for a moment, "that Ricky can't eat with us."
Jane concurred. "Mr. Towne generally is by all accounts an exceptionally bustling individual."
Adelaide conveyed a little cloth fan with gold-lacquered sticks. At the point when she talked she kept her eyes upon the fan. "Do you generally call him 'Mr. Towne'?"
"Obviously."
"Yet, not when you're distant from everyone else."
Jane flushed. "Indeed, I do. What difference would it make?"
"Yet, my dear, it is so exceptionally formal. Furthermore, you will wed him."
"He said that he had told you."
"Ricky lets me know everything. We are exceptionally lifelong companions, you know."
Jane didn't say anything. There was, for sure, nothing to say. She was not at all envious of Adelaide. She pondered, obviously, why Towne ought to have ignored this wonderful woman to pick a pitiful kid. However, he had picked the kid, and that settled it to the extent that Mrs. Laramore was concerned.
Yet, it didn't settle it for Adelaide. "I think it is unmistakably entertaining for you to call him 'Mr. Towne.' Poor

Ricky! You mustn't hold him at a careful distance."
"Same difference either way."
"Indeed, none of us have," said Adelaide, intentionally.
Jane gazed toward her. "Most of you? What do you mean, Mrs. Laramore?"
"Gracious, the ladies that Ricky has cherished," gently.
The breezes shuddered the strips of Jane's dress, vacillating her unsettles. The peacock on the grass expressed a conflicting note. Jane was subliminally mindful of a connection among Adelaide and the shined bird. She discussed the peacock.
"What a repulsive voice he has."
Adelaide gazed. "Who?"
"The peacock," said Jane.
Then Eloise and Edith came in, and as of now the men, and Lucy and Del from an excursion to the little porkers, and Adelaide going out with Del to supper was awkwardly mindful that Jane had either naively or cunningly wouldn't examine with her the ones who had been cherished by Frederick Towne!
The supper was tasty. "Our ranch items," Delafield bragged. Indeed, even the fish, it appeared, he had found that morning, motoring over to the stream and taking them back to be parted and seared and presented with minimal new potatoes. There was chicken and asparagus, little cream cheeses with the serving of mixed greens, loaded up berries in a Royal Worcester bowl, roses from the nursery. "All local," said the pleased new spouse.

Jane ate with little craving. She wouldn't examine with Adelaide the previous heart undertakings of her pledged, yet the words rang in her ears, "The ladies that Ricky has cherished."

Jane was youthful. Furthermore, to youth, love is for endless time periods. The prospect of herself as one of a progression of Dulcineas was debasing. She was fretful and miserable. It was pointless to guarantee herself that Towne had picked her over the remainder. She was not sufficiently modern to expect that it is, maybe, better to take care of business' last love than his first. That Towne had made it feasible for any lady him as Adelaide talked, appeared to Jane to drag her own connection to him in the residue.

The strength of the breeze expanded. The table was protected by the house, however finally Delafield chose, "We would be wise to go in. The downpour is coming. We can have our espresso in the corridor."

Their leaving had the impact of a charge. Huge drops sprinkled into the plates. The men, workers and servants hurried to the salvage of china and material.

The curtains of the ladies spilled in the breeze. Adelaide's tulle was a pennant of green and blue. The peacock came quickly up the walk, crying rambunctiously, and tracked down a shielded spot underneath the means. From the wide lobby, they saw the downpour in silver sheets. Then, at that point, the entryways were closed against the beating wind.

They drank their espresso, and scaffold tables were taken. There were enough without Jane to frame two tables. Furthermore, she was happy. She meandered into the parlor and twisted herself up in a seat by the window. The window opened in the yard. Past the white points of support she could see the street, and the downpour soaked garden.

After a period the downpour halted, and the world showed totally obvious against the opal brilliance of the western sky. The peacock emerged from his stowing away spot, and hauled a weighty tail over the drenched grass.

It was cool and the air was sweet. Jane lay with her head against a pad, watching out. The fact that Towne would come makes her hopeless and wanted. Maybe in his presence her questions would evaporate. It developed dim and more obscure. Jane shut her eyes and finally she nodded off.

She was woken by Towne's voice. He was on the patio. "Where could everyone be?"

It was Adelaide who responded to him. "They have motored into Alexandria to the films. Eloise would have it. In any case, I remained — sitting tight for you, Ricky."

"Where's Jane?"

"She went up-steps early. Like a sluggish kid."

Jane heard his snicker. "She is a youngster — a sweetheart kid."

Then, at that point, in the obscurity Adelaide said, "Don't, Ricky."

"What difference would it make?"

"Do you recollect that some time ago you called me — a sweetheart kid?"
"Did I? Indeed, maybe you were. You are positively an extremely beguiling lady."
Jane, listening energetically, guaranteed herself that obviously he was amiable. He must be.
Adelaide was talking. "So you will declare it to-morrow?"
"Who told you?"
"Edith."
"Indeed, it appeared to be ideal, Adelaide. The big day isn't too distant and the world should know it."
A quiet second, then, "Goodness, Ricky, Ricky!"
"Adelaide! Try not to take it like that."
"I can't resist. You are leaving my life. What's more, you've forever been major areas of strength for so, large, and daring. No one else will at any point match you."
At the point when he talked, his voice had a new and milder note. "I didn't dream it would hurt you."
"You could have known."
The lightning glinting along the skyline showed Adelaide remaining close to Towne's seat.
"Ricky" — the murmured words arrived at Jane — "kiss me once — to bid farewell.'"

## Section XXVIII

## IN THE PINE GROVE

It was when Jane had told Baldy: "I feel like a childish pig."
"Why, my dear?"
"To take your valuable award before it is cold. It is not exactly right."
"It's anything but an issue of right or wrong. On the off chance that things

turn out with these new individuals as I trust, I'll paint like distraught for the following two months. Furthermore, you'll have a difficult, but not impossible task ahead like my model. They like you, Jane. They said as much."

He had driven on consistently for a period, and had then said, "I never believed you should wed him."

"Why not, Baldy?"

He turned his illuminated eyes upon her. "Janey — I believed that you should have your — dreams — — "

She had laid her hand on his arm in a quick stroke. "You're a sweetheart — — " and inevitably, "Nothing can take us from one another, ever, Baldy."

Never had they moved nearer in soul than as of now. Yet, they said very little regarding it. At the point when they came to the house, Baldy went on the double to the carport. "I'll answer that letter, and put in a decent evening time investigating my representations." He didn't tell her how dark the day extended in front of him — that brilliant day which had begun with high expectations.

Jane changed to a free straight dress of orange cotton, and without a cap, feeling real opportunity in the breaking of her bonds, she swung along the way to the little forest. It was sweet-smelling with the warm fragrance of the pines, and there was a cool shade in the core of it. Jane had carried a sack of stockings to patch, and plunked down to her plain errand, grinning a little as she thought about the differentiation between this evening and yesterday, when she had sat on the edge of the wellspring and watched Adelaide and the peacock. She had no sensation of malice against Adelaide. She knew exclusively of incredible gratitude. She was, to be sure, right now, saturated with divine substance. Here was where she should have been. She had a feeling of a happy break. Merrymaid descended the way, her tail a crest. The cat followed. A bronze butterfly drifted across their vision, and they jumped for it — yet it went above them — euphorically towards the open blue of the sky. The two felines looked after it, then, at that point, created themselves cautiously like a couple of small scale lions — their paws before them, languid peered toward yet alert for additional butterflies, or for Jane's bustling string.

What's more, it was hence that Towne was viewed as her. Persuaded that the house was vacant, he had begun towards Baldy's studio. Then down the vista of the pine woods, his eye had been gotten by a spot of brilliant variety. He had followed it.

She set out her work and gazed toward him. "You shouldn't have come."

"My dear youngster, no difference either way. Jane, you are making piles of molehills."

"I'm not."

He plunked down close to her. The little felines drew away, far fetched. "It was normal that you ought to have loathed it. What's more, a thing like that is difficult for a man to make sense of. Without appearing to be a — scoundrel — — "

"There is nothing to make sense of."
"Be that as it may, there is. I have made you miserable, and I'm heartbroken."
She shook her head, and talked nicely. "I assume I am — blissful. Mr. Towne, your reality isn't my reality. I like straightforward things and wonderful things, and genuine things. What's more, I like a One-Woman man, Mr. Towne."
He attempted to chuckle. "You are desirous."
"No," she said, unobtrusively, "it isn't so much that, despite the fact that men like you think it is. A lady who has a sense of pride should realize her significant other has her regard. Her heart should rest in him."
He talked gradually. "I'll concede that I've philandered a great deal. Yet, I've never needed to wed anybody yet. I can guarantee you my future."
"Please accept my apologies. In any case, regardless of whether the previous evening had never been — I figure I ought to have — surrendered you. I had started to feel that I didn't cherish you. That out there in Chicago you deeply inspired me. Mr. Towne, I am grieved. Furthermore, I am thankful. For all your graciousness — — " She flushed and went on, "You know, obviously, that I shan't be content until — I don't owe you anything...."
He laid his hand on hers. "I wish you wouldn't discuss it. It was nothing."
"It was an extraordinary arrangement."
He peered down at her, slim and youthful and limitlessly alluring. "You

shouldn't even need to think I will let you go," he said.
"I'm apprehensive — you should — — "
He blazed out of nowhere. "I'm to a greater degree a One-Woman man as opposed to you think. In the event that you will not wed me, I will not have any other person. I'll continue alone. Concerning Adelaide — — A lady like that doesn't expect considerably more than I gave. That is all I can say regarding her. She makes no difference to me, truly, and never will. She plays the game, and so do I, yet all at once it's just a game."
He looked drained and old. "I'll travel to another country to-morrow. At the point when I return, maybe you'll alter your perspective."
"I won't ever transform it," she said, "never."
He stood up. "Jane, I could fulfill you." He held her hand as she remained adjacent to him.
She took a gander at him and realized that he proved unable. Her fantasies had returned to her — of Galahad — of Robin Hood ... the universe of sentiment had again flung wide its gates....
After Towne had gone she sat for quite a while thoroughly considering it. She accused herself. She had broken her commitment. However, he, as well, had broken a commitment.
She wrapped up repairing the stockings, and folded them into minimal balls. The little felines were sleeping — the shadows were loosened up and the sun skewed through the pines. She ate to get, for

her return had been startling, and Sophy had not been advised.
She could have brought to the possibility of her undertakings some weak sensation of disappointment. Be that as it may, she had none. She was happy to go in — to make an omelet — and cream the potatoes — and have hot bread rolls and berries — and honey.
Arranging accordingly, capability, she raised her eyes — to see going along the way the two young men who had of late been Evans' nearby sidekicks. She addressed them as they contacted her. "Mightn't you at any point remain for a moment? I'll make you some lemonade."
They halted and checked out at her such that frightened her. "We can't," Arthur said; "we're heading toward the Follettes. We figured we could help."
She gazed at them. "Help? Your meaning could be a little more obvious."
Sandy wheezed. "Goodness, didn't you notice? Mrs. Follette kicked the bucket this morning...."

## Part XXIX

## JANE DREAMS

Evans had tracked down his mom around early afternoon, lying on the love seat at the foot of her bed. He had remained at home in the first part of the day to help her, and at ten o'clock she had gone up-steps to rest a piece before lunch. Old Mary had called her, and she had not replied. So Evans had gone into her space to find that she had gotten away calmly from the world wherein she misrepresented her own significance. It would happen

without her. She had not been friendly however the neighbors would all come and feel for her child. Furthermore, they would miss her, since she had added to the local area some proportion of impressiveness, which they appreciated even as they loathed it.
Evans had attempted to get Baldy on the phone, yet proved unable. Jane was at Grass Hills. He would call up at a significant distance later. There was not an obvious explanation for why he ought to ruin them this day of days. So he had done the things that must be finished in the shadowed house. Dr. Hallam came, and others. Evans saw them and they disappeared. He moved in a fantasy. He had nobody to sympathize with personally his distress — no sister, no sibling, nobody, aside from his little canine, who followed behind him, contemplative looked at, and with limping steps.
The entirety of what had happened didn't come to him immediately. He had an inclination that at any second his mom could clear in from the out-of-entryways, in her white material and level dark cap, and find a seat at the top of the table, and let him know the fresh insight about the morning.
He had no lunch, so old Mary fixed a plate for him. He didn't eat, however drank some milk. Then he and Rusty took up their fretful meandering through the quiet rooms. Old Mary, consistent with custom, had drawn every one of the blinds and shut large numbers of the windows, so the house was loaded up with a kind of brilliant

despair. Evans went into his mom's little office on the main floor, and took a seat at her work area. It was in line, and spread out on the blotting surface was the composing paper with the brilliant peak, and the case of brilliant seals. Also, he had chuckled at her! He recalled with an ache that they could at absolutely no point in the future chuckle together. He was distant from everyone else.
He asked why such things occurred. Was all of life as vile as this? Must one generally track down misfortune every step of the way of the street? He had lost his childhood, had lost Jane. Furthermore, presently his mom. Was all that to be removed? Could there be nothing left except for solidarity to persevere?
Indeed, God helping him, he would persevere to the end....
He shut the work area tenderly and went out into the obscured lobby. As he followed its length, an entryway opened toward the end. Dark against the brilliance of the past, he saw the two fellows. They approached with some delay, however when they saw his drained face, they failed to remember hesitance.
"We recently heard. Also, we need to help." Sandy was representative.
Arthur was stunned. Yet, he grasped Evans' sleeve and gazed toward him. His eyes expressed out loud whatever his voice declined.
Evans, with his arms across their shoulders, attracted the young men to him. "It was great of you to come."
"Miss Barnes said," again it was Sandy who talked, "that maybe we

could get some pine from the little forest. That your mom enjoyed it."
"Miss Barnes? Might it be said that she is back? Is she aware?"
"We told her. She is coming directly home."
Baldy drove Jane in his little vehicle. As she entered she appeared to acquire the light with her. She lit up the house like a light.
She strolled quickly towards Evans, and held out her hand. "My dear, I am so grieved."
"I thought you were at Grass Hills."
"We returned out of the blue."
"I am so happy — you came."
He was making some terrible memories with his voice. He was unable to go on....
Jane addressed the young men. "Did you get some information about the pine branches? Simply those, and roses from the nursery, Evans."
"You generally consider things — — "
"Baldy will take the young men to the woods, and do any tasks you might have for him." She was her quiet and capable self — allowing him to deal with his feelings while she coordinated others.
Baldy, coming in, wrung Evans' hand. "The young men and I will get the pine, and Edith Towne is emerging to help. I hit her up to tell her — — "
Baldy halted at that. He was unable to talk here of the brilliance that enveloped him. He had said, "Assuming demise ought to come to us, Edith! Does anything more count?" And she had said, "Nothing." And presently she was coming and they would pick roses together in the

nursery. Furthermore, love and life would priest to a more prominent mystery....

At the point when Baldy and the young men had gone, Jane and Evans opened the windows and pulled up the shades. The house was loaded up with clear light, and was cool in the breeze.

At the point when they had gotten done, Jane said, "That is all, I think. We can rest a little. What's more, as of now it will be the ideal opportunity for supper."

"I need no supper."

They were in the library. Outside was an amethyst nightfall, with a youthful moon low overhead. Evans and Jane remained by the window, watching out, and Jane asked in a quieted voice, "You need no supper since she will not be at the opposite finish of the table?"

"Indeed." His face was abandoned by her. His hands were secured. His throat was dry. Briefly he wanted to be separated from everyone else that he could sob for his mom.

And afterward Jane said, "Let me sit at the opposite end of your table."

He turned around to her, and saw her eyes, and what he saw compelled him to connect indiscriminately for her hand — compassion, delicacy — a womanly agonizing delicacy.

"Goodness, Evans, Evans," she said, "I won't wed Frederick Towne."

"Why not?" thickly.

"I don't cherish him."

"Do you cherish me, Jane?"

She gestured and couldn't talk. They stuck together. He sobbed and was not embarrassed about it.

Also, remaining there, with his head against her bosom, Jane realized that she had been viewed as the best. Marriage was not a thing of extravagance and delicate living, of flaring snapshots of wild inclination. It was a thing of hardness shared, of soul meeting soul, of dream matching dream. Jane, that evening, had paused to rest as she had come into the obscured lobby, and had seen Evans remaining between those thin chaps. So sometime in the future, maybe, in this old house — his children!

www.ingramcontent.com/pod-product-compliance
Lightning Source LLC
LaVergne TN
LVHW012042160826
845678LV00014B/2676

* 9 7 9 8 8 4 6 7 3 2 2 7 8 *